We Have His Promise

ALTON WEDEL

SERMONS FOR THE
SUNDAYS AFTER PENTECOST
(SUNDAYS IN ORDINARY TIME)
LAST THIRD

CYCLE C GOSPEL TEXTS

C.S.S. Publishing Co., Inc.
Lima, Ohio

WE HAVE HIS PROMISE

Copyright © 1988 by
The C.S.S. Publishing Company, Inc.
Lima, Ohio

All rights reserved. No part of this publication may be reproduced, stored in a retrieval system, or transmitted in any form or by any means, electronic, mechanical, photocopying, recording, or otherwise, without the prior permission of the publisher. Inquiries should be addressed to: The C.S.S. Publishing Company, Inc., 628 South Main Street, Lima, Ohio 45804.

LIBRARY OF CONGRESS
Library of Congress Cataloging-in-Publication Data

Wedel, Alton F.
    We have His promise: sermons for the Sundays after Pentecost: last third (Sundays in ordinary time): cycle C Gospel texts / Alton F. Wedel.
      p. cm.
    ISBN 1-556-73057-8
    1. God — Promises — Sermons. 2. Bible. N.T. Gospels — Sermons. 3. Church year sermons. 4. Sermons, American. I. Title.
BT180.P7W43 1988
252'.6—dc19
                                              88-1513
                                                    CIP

8854 / ISBN 1-55673-057-8   PRINTED IN U.S.A.

Table of Contents

About the Author	6
Preface	7
Lectionary Preaching After Pentecost	9
Proper 23[1] Pentecost 21[2] Ordinary Time 28[3]	*The Day You Were Healed* 11 *Luke 17:11-19*
Proper 24 Pentecost 22 Ordinary Time 29	*Lord, I Believe — Or Do I?* 19 *Luke 18:1-8*[1,3] *Luke 18:1-8*[2]
Proper 25 Pentecost 23 Ordinary Time 30	*An Encounter With Two Old Friends* 27 *Luke 18:9-14*
Proper 26 Ordinary Time 31	*The Gospel of the Little Man* 35 *Luke 19:1-10*
Reformation Sunday[2]	*Emancipation Proclamation* 43 *John 8:31-36*
All Saints' Sunday[1]	*The Sermon on the Level* 50 *Luke 6:20-36*
All Saints' Sunday[2] All Saints' Day[3]	*Heaven Can't Wait* 58 *Matthew 5:1-12*
Proper 27 Pentecost 25 Ordinary Time 32	*Are There Any Questions?* 66 *Luke 20:27-38*
Proper 28 Pentecost 26 Ordinary Time 33	*How to Stay on Top of It* 75 *Luke 21:5-19*

Pentecost 27[2]   *Advancers Over Decliners*   82
                                          Luke 19:11-27

Christ the King[1]   *Christ is King*   89
                                          John 12:9-19

Christ the King[2,3]   *Believing is Seeing*   96
                                          Luke 23:35-43

Thanksgiving Eve / Day   *One Nation, Under Mercy*   102
                                          Luke 17:11-19

[1] Common Lectionary
[2] Lutheran Lectionary
[3] Roman Catholic Lectionary

About the Author

Dr. Alton F. Wedel, born the son of a Lutheran pastor in rural Wisconsin, began his pursuit of the ministry at Concordia College, Milwaukee, and in theological studies at Concordia Seminary, Saint Louis, where he was graduated in 1945. He continued graduate studies at the same seminary in Systematics and Biblical Theology, and in Old Testament theology during a period of residence at the Ecumenical Institute, Tantur, Jerusalem, Israel. His honorary Doctor of Divinity degree was conferred by the Saint Louis seminary in 1969.

Now retired to a ministry of writing and teaching and community service in Naples, Florida, Pastor Wedel served 42 years as a pastor of the church, including in his duties extensive service on national church boards and committees. His parish pastorates afforded experience in rural congregations of West Canada, in small towns of the Gogebic Iron Range in Upper Michigan, in a smaller city on the Bootheel of Southern Missouri, and for the major portion in a large suburban parish of Saint Louis and a central city church in Minneapolis.

With his spouse of 42 years, Mim, he enjoys the blessing of three children — Dr. Mark, a member of the American Fellowship of Chest Physicians who is working in critical care at the Scripps Clinic in San Diego; Kathi, an internationally known design artist and Registered Nurse and spouse of a Milwaukee pastor; and Tim, an artist in Grand Junction, Colorado. Six children, to whom this little work is dedicated, claim him and his spouse as grandparents.

Pastor Wedel sends this book of sermons on its mission with the prayer that the promise may be the strong foundation of the faith for all who read.

Preface

We have his promise, one unfolding on another. I will never leave you or forsake you. Nothing can separate you from my love. I have come that you might have life and have it abundantly. Ask, and you shall receive; seek, and you shall find; knock, and the door is opened. The Kingdom of God is at hand. The rule of God is within you. Come to me, and I will give you rest. He who drinks of the living water will never thirst again. In my Father's house I will prepare a place for you, and come again. He who believes in me has everlasting life.

The Bible is the Book of Promise. Of all the images that people entertain of Holy Scripture, this is its foremost character and message. If God is for us, and if God is with us, who can be against us, what can threaten us, and prevail?

The seed of the promise was formed in the loving heart of our eternal God before the foundations of the earth were laid. It was planted in the footsteps of a fallen Adam in the garden. Its buds appeared with Abraham and Moses and King David in the covenant. The prophets cultivated it. The Psalmists sang of it. And at length it came to full bloom in the fulness of the time in Jesus Christ in whom all the promises of God are yea and amen.

Forty years of promise preaching in the parish ministry have been closed down since I agreed some months ago to offer on these pages echoes of the promise as I hear them now. The promise was the same throughout the years, but in the changing time and circumstance of life, the word of promise came with fresh grace every morning. As one of those strange characters who wrote in full each Sunday homily, I now own within six feet of my right arm four drawers full of files that represent each one of those short years. They are saturated to the dripping point with promise, cross, and resurrection.

Yet there is not a single one of them that would tolerate a rerun. On occasion, when I checked the file to find a shortcut through the shadow of next Sunday's sermon, the file was disappointing. The parables of Jesus, his discourses, the prophetic and the apostolic word, the record of the mighty acts of God could not be canned in sermons for reuse at later times. The dynamic of the Word had blown the lid off.

The sermons in this little booklet, then, will serve no purpose but to share the Word of Promise as one person heard it in the recent months. If, as an accessory, they stimulate exclusive promise preaching in our church, my gratitude will not be measured. As one who now spends more worship time in padded pews than in the pontiff's pulpit, I can tell you what I need to hear. The promise!

Alton F. Wedel
Naples, Florida

Lectionary Preaching After Pentecost

Virtually all pastors who make use of the sermons in this book will find their worship life and planning shaped by one of two lectionary series. Most mainline Protestant denominations have now approved — either for provisional or official use — the three- year Common (Consensus) Lectionary. This family of denominations includes United Methodist, Presbyterian, United Church of Christ, Episcopal, and Disciples of Christ.

Lutherans and Roman Catholics, while testing the Common Lectionary on a limited basis at present, follow their own three-year cycle of texts. While there are divergences between the Common and Lutheran/Roman Catholic system, the gospel texts show striking parallels, with few text selections evidencing significant differences. Virtually all the gospel texts included in this book will, therefore, be applicable to worship and preaching planning for clergy following either lectionary.

A significant divergence does occur, however, in the method by which specific gospel texts are assigned to specific calendar days. The Common and Roman Catholic Lectionaries accomplish this by counting backward from Christ the King (Last Sunday after Pentecost), discarding "extra" texts from the front of the list; Lutherans follow the opposite pattern, counting forward from The Holy Trinity, discarding "extra" texts at the end of the list.

The following index will aid the user of this book in matching the right text to the right Sunday during the "Pentecost Half" of the church year (days listed here include only those appropriate to this book's content):

Fixed-date Lectionaries		*Lutheran Lectionary*
Common	**Roman Catholic**	
Proper 23 *October 9-15*	Ordinary Time 28	Pentecost 21
Proper 24 *October 16-22*	Ordinary Time 29	Pentecost 22

Proper 25 *October 23-29*	Ordinary Time 30	Pentecost 23
Proper 26 *October 30 — November 5*	Ordinary Time 31	Pentecost 24
All Saints' Sunday	All Saints' Day	All Saints' Sunday
Proper 27 *November 6-12*	Ordinary Time 32	Pentecost 25
Proper 28 *November 13-19*	Ordinary Time 33	Pentecost 26
		Pentecost 27
Christ the King	Christ the King	Christ the King
Thanksgiving	Thanksgiving	Thanksgiving

Luke 17:11-19

Proper 23 (C)
Pentecost 21 (L)
Ordinary Time 28 (RC)

The Day You Were Healed

That was a good day, wasn't it, the day you were healed, when your physician wrote your exit visa from the hospital, when the nurses wheeled you to the front door where your spouse was waiting in the family limo, and you were on your way? Almost forgotten now is the pain, the apprehension, and the helplessness that you had felt when the paramedics brought you in with siren screaming, the intravenous feedings, the wires and the tubes that made you feel like an electrical appliance. Almost forgotten, too is your whispered "Lord, have mercy," your wondering whether you would make it, the concern on faces of your loved ones, the pastor's prayers, the healing promise of the Lord that he had spoken at your bedside. That was a good day, wasn't it, the day when you were healed?

On arrival home you told your friends and family how fortunate you were, how the doctor said that if you had not been in good shape otherwise, you probably could not have made it, how the discipline of jogging and aerobics had paid off. You drew a long deep breath and said, "Thank the Lord."

But did I hear you say, "The Lord"? After several days or weeks of convalescence you might get back to church again and nod to God, as is our habit, with a gesture of thanksgiving. For the moment you could isolate him in the closet with your other good luck charms until another desperate need arose and you would have to polish up your lines again, "Jesus, Master, have mercy!"

On Credits and Debits

How can we explain it, that when these ten lepers had received the gift of healing, nine neglected gratitude to him who healed them? Or how do we account for this when we are healed, that God gets little more than casual recognition, an incidental "Thank the Lord," while our personal fitness or the skill of medics or our high tech progress draw the commendation? Or how do we defend the notion that the good gifts of the Father's kindly hand are listed as our human right, while the Giver of the gifts is thoughtlessly ignored? Someone has said that God is credited with every hook and slice along life's fairway, while we take credit for the hole-in-one.

One need not page around the Bible very long to find it — the prevailing "Master of my house" approach to life that shifts the credits from God's side to ours and the debits from our side to God's. King David, grasping destiny in his own hands, became proud above his people, turned aside from the commandments, and exposed a leprosy of heart more hideous than leprosy of skin. King Uzziah, when he was strong, grew proud to his destruction, usurping rights of temple priests in burning incense at the altar. He was smitten by the Lord with leprosy that forced him from the temple for the balance of his life.

For all the glowing tribute that we pay the virtues of thanksgiving and humility, expressed in our complete dependence on a power not our own, is it not our strength that took us through and our good shape that helped us make it? Or was it not the surgeon's skill, the advances of technology, the mechanics of science? Is not the produce of the land our own, without the sun and soil chemistry, because we have degrees in agriculture, and the latest methods, and machinery, and herbicides, and pesticides? Is it not our own capacity for work and our long hours in the field that are responsible for our success?

Scarcely do we think of God as the giver of our gifts, or the healer of our diseases, or even as the forgiver of our iniquities. What gifts do we have that have not been earned? What has God done about malaria, or polio, or smallpox? These nearly-obsolete diseases, in America at least, are exhibits of the human genius. What has God done about our coronaries, AIDS, or cancers? What has he done about the hungry Ethiopian? Or what iniquities require his forgiveness? Do we mean to say there are iniquities to be forgiven? Seldom do our lives become a high doxology of praise to anybody but ourselves, or to someone just as mortal and as helpless and dependent as ourselves. The froth of pious praise to God does not befit our self-esteem.

The Nauseous Horror

Leprosy was a nauseous horror. There was little back in Bible days to equal it for that completely hopeless feeling. To describe it in detail might be a little more than we can handle at this hour of the morning. And to detail the leper's situation as the human outcast, confined not in aseptic isolation wards or nursing homes, but in the dirty caves and off the beaten paths, separated from family, synagogue, and friends — that might be more than our enlightened sense of sympathy could tolerate, for we have learned much better ways of isolating people. But Luke, who was himself a doctor and a partner of the good physician brings us face-to-face with the realities by simply telling us that these ten lepers suffered from the horror. Somewhere near the border of Samaria and Galilee, as Jesus journeyed to Jerusalem, he heard the plea for help that bridged the distance they were forced by law to keep between themselves and others. "Jesus, Master, have mercy on us!"

The Spark of Faith and Hope

Whether they were prompted in their plea for mercy by a momentary spark of faith, or whether this was one last shot in the darkness of their living hell, I doubt that we can say. People go to great lengths in search of help in hopeless situations. Some years ago, while serving a small parish near the southern border of Missouri, I traveled weekly to a tiny rural church in Arkansas where Sunday after Sunday the same faces of the faithful could be seen at worship. Suddenly I noted visitors appearing at the worship and discovered that they came from many distant places to the nearby town where a publicized but questioned treatment was administered for cancer. That treatment represented one last hope, however faint. And so it was for these ten lepers also, that in Jesus, rumored as a wonder worker, they grasped for one last hope. But this is certain, that when Jesus said, "Go and show yourselves to the priests," they hit the road with nothing but his word, even with their flesh still rotting with the leprosy. And as they went, they were cleansed.

No magic touch . . . no potent potient . . . no wonder drug . . . Only the Word. Jesus had not treated them in their disease. He had healed them. And this was a good day for the lepers, this day when they were healed.

Sometimes One Last Hope

We can never give up hope. Although we have added to the list of terminals, and though a few diseases still remain with no known cure, the human genius has made strides of progress through research and treatment. The time and wisdom of our scientific sages still continues in our laboratories all around the world in search of treatments for the endless list of human ills — hypertension, heart disease, diabetes, carcinoma, addictions, AIDS, Alzheimer's, disorders of the mind, multiple sclerosis, or whatever is your personal plague. We haven't got time for the pain, and it was God himself who said it, was it not, when he came down from heaven to survey the miracles and wonders of humanity: "This is only the beginning of what these possibility thinkers will do."

We cannot stand by while the human family suffers. We cannot hoard the gifts of God while others hunger. We cannot turn aside when someone hurts. The burden of an agonized humanity is on our hearts, and we respond with prayers and gifts, with dollars for research, with bread for hungry children, and with our presence in compassion at the side of someone close to us in trial. We can never give up hope.

But sometimes there is one last hope — hope discovered not in looking forward to a wonder cure, but in turning backward to the one who heals. When an anxious family has to hear what seems to be the final word, "I'm sorry. There is nothing we can do," the final word remains with God. And please note carefully, the Word of God is never final.

It is a truism that we are living in a world of sickness, death, and separation from our healing God. And when the sickness is our own, when it is our death on its approach, we look for miracles. Often God says "No." But that no is not the final word. We have his promise of a day when suffering, pain and death will be no more, when tears are dried, and when our voices blend in alleluias at the throne of him in whom the new creation has been fully realized. He who came to heal will heal in ways our highest hope could never realize. Threescore years and ten, a little more, a little less, is not the total of our lives. The great shalom is yet to come.

The company of faith, therefore, cannot abandon healing ministry or pass it off to others by default. As we walk the footsteps of the Master, compassion is the very essence of our being, and in that compassion we can be the light that shines in the tunnel of despair and darkness for our suffering fellows. That light, shaped as a cross, spells hope when all is hopeless. We have the promise, and as all his promises have ripened to fulfillment, the promise of his life instead of death, his peace instead of fear, is certain.

One Turned Back

"Then one of them, when he saw that he was healed, turned back, praising God with a loud voice; and he fell on his face at Jesus' feet, giving him thanks. Now he was a Samaritan." The differences between Samaritans and Jews, differences which seemed to have dissolved within the bondage of their leprosy, now reappeared. Age-old differences of race and nationality, religion, sex, or age, or whatever we invent to climb a ladder rung above another in the human family, had melted in this company of beggars. The signs of separation in the human family that plague us still had faded. Their common need, their common crisis, their common condemnation to a common death, their common cry for mercy leveled them as beggars just as we together share the isolation that has separated us from God and stand together in our need for healing. But the difference! "Were there not ten cleansed? Where are the nine? Was no one found to return and give praise to God except this foreigner?"

What was the difference? All of these afflicted, desperate folk had cried for mercy. All obeyed the word of Jesus as, with no sign that their plea was heard, they hurried off to see the priests. They were ready to begin the detailed ritual of cleansing given in remote Leviticus, the complicated liturgy for cleansing lepers and restoring them to their communities and families.

But the lone Samaritan had little taste for liturgy except the liturgy of thanks and praise to him whose word had cleansed. He had little interest in the priestly health officials, for his cleansing had not come from them, but prompted by the mercy he had asked for and received, his impelling interest was in him who healed.

The Gift Without the Giver is Bare

That's the difference. And in the Gospel as Saint Luke

records it, a central message is that in Christ Jesus God has given to the world his healing touch, and that the world would glorify and praise the God of heaven and earth because his grace is given us in Christ. This Samaritan had recognized the glory of the Lord revealed in Jesus Christ. He saw that God was in Christ Jesus, for as he fell at Jesus' feet, he praised God. And it was a good day for this lone Samaritan, this day when he was healed. "Rise and go your way; your faith has made you well."

In the Midrashim, the Jewish commentaries on the ancient Scriptures written by the learned Jewish rabbis, we can find instruction for the leper. He had to bring before the priest a branch of cedar and a sprig of hyssop, confessing that while he had been proud like cedar, he would henceforth be as humble as the lowly hyssop.* And we recall the Psalm of David who in his penitential plea, as he recalled his sin against Uriah and Bathsheba and a host of others, cried, "Cleanse me with hyssop and I shall be clean. Wash me, and I shall be as white as snow." He begged for healing, for cleansing, and for restoration to the intimate relationship with God that he once knew but now had severed. And he remembered his good day of healing, "I will confess my transgression to the Lord; then thou didst forgive the guilt of my sin."

Christ is Our Health

The healed Samaritan should not be used to illustrate a primer lesson on remembering to say thank you, or to stir up guilt in little children who forget. This is the Gospel of the grace of God that took on flesh and blood in Jesus Christ through whom we are restored and cleansed and healed, made whole again, and holy in his sight. The Giver is himself the gift. Our need is not for his forgiveness, or his cleansing, or his healing, only to go forth and sin again, and dirty up again,

---

* See *Biblical Archaeology Review*, September/October 1986, Vol. XII, No. 5, page 39 for an account of the leper's cleansing as described in the Midrashim.

and take on other sicknesses again. Our need is Christ himself, for Christ is our wholeness, Christ is our health.

It was a good day, wasn't it, the day when we were healed, when we found in Christ the mercy of our God, when our self-insistence and self-righteousness was drained by our confession, "God, be merciful to me," and when our prayer was answered by the gift he gave in his own Son? In Christ who is our health we are brought back from the pits and reinstated as the children of the Father and as members of his family. It was a good day — not because our self-esteem had been destroyed, but because it was restored; nor because the props beneath us had collapsed, but because our feet were planted on the solid rock again; not because we had a claim on him, but because in mercy he had laid his claim on us.

Life as High Doxology

When we are healed and cleansed, made whole, restored, then life becomes a high doxology of praise, not only as a hymn of thankfulness to sing, but as the motif of our days. From that day forward we will recognize the one who heals all our diseases, who forgives all our iniquities, who gives the sunshine and the rain and blesses us with bread, the one who stands with us in grief and warms us with his presence. We will know that life is lived within the everlasting arms of love, and nothing can isolate us from his love, not even death. We live in his intensive care. We have the promise.

Luke 18:1-8 (C, RC) *Proper 24 (C)*
Luke 18:1-8a(L) *Pentecost 22 (L)*
  Ordinary Time 30 (RC)

Lord, I Believe — Or Do I?

In his ministry of teaching, Jesus was a master at the art of storytelling. Many of his stories, known as parables, have been our favorites through the years since first we heard them. They can be repeated many times, and we will never tire of them — the story of the Good Samaritan, the prodigal, the two men praying in the temple, the sower in the field. And the lessons that the Master taught in parables are pointed, holding up for our inspection virtues to be practiced, vices to avoid, relationships to be cultivated, and especially his promise to believe.

His promise cloaked in parables is most important. The burden that the parables of Jesus carry is much weightier than little tidbits of morality or vice or virtue. Their concern is not so much with our behavior and what we are up to as they are with God's behavior and what he is up to. They bring the promise of the Gospel of the kingdom and impel response. They lay the kingdom claim upon our hearts and lives and impel us to submit. They have a way of pricking like a needle at those tender places where our weakness and our need for healing is most obvious. They speak assurance when the going is most rough. They stamp the guarantee of love eternal when the prospects are most dim.

But the parables cannot be mastered. They cannot be heard or read like Aesop's fables with the casual concern that says, "I've heard that one before. What's new?" They refuse to be defused, for unlike a land mine that is detonated only once, the parables are detonated every time we step on them. The parable may be the same, but in kaleidoscopic fashion the design is changed with every turn of time. The word it brings us in the here-and-now will be quite different from the word it brought us in the there-and-then.

So it is with this one, The Parable of the Unrighteous Judge, or the Parable of the Persistent Widow, or the Parable of Persevering Prayer, or the Parable of Tenacious Faith. It has been known by all these names. But today the major message waits for this last line, the one so frequently ignored, sometimes omitted altogether, "When the Son of man comes, will he find faith on the earth?"

The Promise

The parable of this unrighteous judge served as a prelude to that question. It was less concerned with telling us to keep on praying than it was with interjecting into our impatience, faithlessness, and hopelessness the promise of the Kingdom, the assurance that though hidden now behind the Cross, the Kingdom will be manifested in the end in all its glory. For, "will not God vindicate his elect, who cry to him day and night? Will he delay long over them? I tell you, he will vindicate them speedily."

In a certain town an unjust judge was on the bench who neither feared the Lord nor cared what people thought of him. His job security did not depend on justice in the courtroom. And a woman in that town who was a widow, assertive and persistent, kept coming back to this unrighteous jurist with her case in which she had received no justice and no settlement, perhaps a money matter, or a problem of inheritance, or an oppression which was common in the lives of widows in those days. She had no recourse other than the court, but in her case the court was useless, for His Honor didn't seem to understand or care. He had no conscience for justice. But the widow kept on coming in the hope that by persistence she could wear him down, and he would have to settle the affair to get her off his neck. Finally, when she had made his nerves raw with her pest-like pleading, he yielded, settled in her favor, vindicated her.

Is God like that? And the Lord said, "Hear what the unrighteous judge says. And will not God vindicate his elect, who cry to him day and night? Will he delay long over them? I tell you, he will vindicate them speedily. Nevertheless, when the Son of man comes, will he find faith on the earth?"

Two caveats as an aside may be in order here. First, with a hint at humor, this is not designed to tell us how to handle judges when we feel that justice handed down has been imperfect. Court costs and attorney fees can be expensive in repeat performances. Appeals are finally exhausted. Even the suggestion that a judge might be unjust can lead to charges of contempt. And secondly, the parable does not imply through this dim picture of the jurist that God is like that, that he has no interest in our case, no concern for justice, and that he has to be cajoled before he listens.

If an unjust scoundrel of a judge will finally do justice, will not God also grant the prayers of his disciples? And if God, whose heart is heavy with compassion for his own, promises their vindication in the end, will he not also be concerned for our undying faithfulness and watchfulness, persistent faith against all odds? "When the Son of man comes, will he find faith on the earth?"

Even When Prayer Seems to Fail

Emmie, a young college student, one day at a game of tennis accidentally discovered on her abdomen a frightening lump that she had never noticed previously. She said nothing to her friends about it, but her fingers constantly moved over it as she worried and she prayed about it. As a week went by, the nodule exploded with growth. Immediate attention was required. After surgery, when pathology had given the bitter word, she cried out as I walked into her room, "They said it's cancer. I don't want to die."

Emmie did not die, for by a miracle that never made the headlines Emmie found her healing, not only freedom from the carcinoma, but the freedom of new faithfulness. Later I would hear her make confession of her momentary faithlessness.

But the miracle we seek may not often be the miracle received, and when bad things happen to good people, reverses that we cannot understand, sudden setbacks in our best-laid plans, we call God to account. The trite and easy answers that we hear about the will of God, or how God doesn't always answer yes, but sometimes no, and other times not yet, these trite and easy answers are small comfort. When it seems our house has been invaded by the powers of evil, when the walls collapse around us, it is difficult to understand or to believe that nothing in creation can seperate us from the love of God in Christ. "When the Son of man comes, will he find faith on the earth?"

From the perspective of passing time it is often possible in faith, however, to see the purposes of God unfold for those who are his own. A young student of medicine, approaching his final year of study, was suddenly laid low with diabetes. The promising career ahead would live within the shadow of the needle and the insulin and the gathering clouds that threaten the diabetic. Then, but one short month into his internship, he was double-whammied by tuberculosis, contracted in his susceptibility in a hospital ward.

But the treatment for a diabetic tubercular patient resulted in what doctors called a miracle. Following his internship and residency, he was given a fellowship in chest medicine, and he went on from there to national board recognition in internal medicine and as a chest physician, and most recently as a specialist in sleep disorders. Though his soul from out the shadow is delivered nevermore, he continues practice in a vital clinic of the West. When it seems that the years of life are telescoped, God can often accomplish more through us in shorter years than in the normal lifetime, whatever that may be. "I tell you, God will vindicate them speedily. Nevertheless, when the Son of man comes, will he find faith on the earth?"

The Long View

The Master's searching question stretches far beyond our faithless moments, beyond our questions, doubts, and answered or unanswered prayers. It has its focus on our Lord's return for judgment and salvation and the vindication of his own. The story of the widow and the judge is a sequel to the teaching that Saint Luke recorded just ahead of this, "The days are coming when you will desire to see one of the days of the Son of man, and you will not see it." The days are coming when you would give anything to see the slightest evidence that God is working out his will and that his purposes are ripening, some sign of kingdom progress, something that would vindicate your mission and your life as his disciple.

John the Baptizer from his prison cell sent word to Jesus, asking, "Are you he that is to come, or shall we look for someone else?" He saw no evidence of anything that might resemble the Messianic kingdom he expected. "Tell John what you see and hear," the Savior answered, "how the blind receive their sight, the lame walk, the lepers are cleansed, the deaf hear, the dead are raised up, and the poor have good news preached to them." The Kingdom that will one day be revealed, when every knee will bend before the sovereign Lord and every tongue confess his holy name, is hidden now, but working surely in the midst of human anguish, among the blind, the deaf, the hungry, the diseased, the war-scarred, the distressed, the dispossessed. The headlines of the daily news point up the darkness and present exhibits of a world possessed by demons. They dismiss the Kingdom claim as nonsense while they sound the trumpet for the human genius that has cures for everything that ails our world. The gospel news points up the light of Christ who is creation's Lord. "When the Son of man comes, will he find faith on earth?"

The days ahead for his disciples were full of peril, trial, persecution, martyrdom — and temptation to give up, toss in the towel, and accept defeat. With this parable Jesus wanted to prepare disciples for the possibility of long delay when patience would be pushed and faith stretched in the stress of mission. But their persistent prayer, "Thy kingdom come," would be answered in his time and in his way. His plan, his purpose, and his end will be accomplished and fulfilled. We have his word for that. Can we believe it? "When the Son of man comes, will he find faith on the earth?"

With confidence born of our Lord's resurrection, his Apostles went to mission, laid their lives on chopping blocks, and hung them on cruel crosses. Their joy was never artificially designed to make an impact on their television viewing audience. They were simply certain that the promise of their Lord would be fulfilled, regardless of adverse conditions, that even in distressful times and often in despair, and frequently in their own failures, the kingdom was at hand. While we might expect them to become a crowd for whom the doom bells toll, they were instead a company who rang the bells of joy around the world. To sample their conviction in the teeth of every peril, read the masterpiece of confidence that Saint Paul penned in 2 Corinthians, chapter 4.

On what foundation did their joy and boldness rest? What mission could have motivated them when all the odds were stacked against them? This little parable of persistent patience illustrates the answer.

We Need the Parable

The church today, not always certain that its Lord knows how to run his business, often tries to run it for him. Not content that all our efforts are not crowned, we crown our own.

Not willing to await the revelation of his kingdom in his time and in his way, we seek to build our little kingdoms now.

When we read the publications, bulletins, releases, and whatever flows from printing presses of the churches, we must be impressed. They speak with hype and hoopla, using words like "lively, joyous, and renewed." Every past event is termed momentous. Every listing on the calendar ahead is called a happening that no one can afford to miss. "Growth has been phenomenal, interest has heightened to a record level, a new spirit has been born," to quote directly. As one follows publications issued from the same source weekly, one can soon determine who will occupy the right hand and the left hand pedestals of glory in the kingdom.

Accentuate the positive, of course. Eliminate the negative. Our merchandising efforts must project the proper image. One does not print the latest verbal scuffle at the meeting of the presbyters, or publicize the drug use in the youth group, or reveal the scandal smoldering between two choir members. Success demands the image of success.

But the Gospel never speaks the language of a merchandising effort. Christ gives us one assurance only, that through the gospel of the cross, his cross and ours, the kingdom would appear. We stand on that assurance. We fasten on that promise. Nothing less will do.

Yet we have often been content with something less. Down through the centuries the church has parroted the prayer, "Thy kingdom come" not always sure of what we ask, sometimes confused on how it comes, or when it comes, or where it comes. We speak about our kingdom building, overhaul the church machinery, rewrite the constitution, initiate new programs, list statistical successes, chart the progress. When the outlook dims, we seek new ways to steady this strange structure we have built on sinking sand. The ark of God does not need human hands to steady it as Uzzah learned when he put up his hand against the ark to steady it as David sought to bring it to Jerusalem, and when the oxen stumbled and the cart began to tip.

Quotations from pop psychology, stories from the *Reader's Digest*, advice for the lovelorn, (and, for shock therapy, a bit of Dr. Ruth) — these can only be the diet of a starved and starving church. We have the promise. Nothing less will do. "When the Son of man comes, will he find faith on the earth?" Or will he find behind the flurry of our busyness a valley of dry bones?

There will be a day — his day, his end. In fact, his day is now, for Christ is in our midst. He keeps company with sinners. He responds with grace to every penitent. He releases captives from the bondage of their Egypt. He takes us by the hand to usher us through those dark shadows into life eternal. In the Gospel of a love that suffered through the death of Calvary we have the promise that our Lord is with us now, and that his kingdom is at hand, and that he will appear again to rule in righteousness and purity forever. That's the word we live on. That's the message of our mission. That's the love that kindles faith and keeps the fire burning. We have his promise.

Luke 18:9-14
Proper 25 (C)
Pentecost 23 (L)
Ordinary Time 30 (RC)

An Encounter With Two Old Friends

We need to exercise our sensitivity today as we encounter two old friends, the Pharisee and the Publican. When I first learned this story in my childhood from the Bible storybook and when I told this story in the early years of ministry, the issue was already cut-and-dried. The righteous Pharisee became the scoundrel whom one loves to hate, while the Publican became the hero.

Recently, however, in the tenor of the times, there has been a subtle shift of accent. The up-front Pharisee is getting better press. The lowly Publican is being more honestly appraised. The story has more depth than it was recognized, and I am less inclined to roller skate across it in my reading of Saint Luke, as though encountering these two old friends could be a casual meeting. Both of them, surprisingly, have taken on new life, and they appear as mirror images of someone whom I know quite well, although not well enough. So as I introduce you to these two old friends again today, you will recognize them, too, though not as bearded characters from Bible days, nor even as contemporaries in your life scene now, but as reflections of the man, the woman, whom you are. In introducing them again, I face the danger of re-creating all the old simplicities and false impressions, or presenting them as tin can targets to be shot at.

First, let me clarify. While the new translations of the Scriptures shun the use of this term "publican," I have a personal problem with the simple title "tax collector." Publican says more than tax collector. For several of my recent years I lived across the street from one who was a tax collector, and while he may have been Republican, he was surely not a publican. He was respected on our block, loved his family, worked hard on the landscape of his property, and was a faithful member of his church. And several years ago when summoned for an audit of 1040, while I went through the jitters, entertained the vision of a hard-nosed auditor, and felt the anger and disgust of having to dig up old records, I found another gentleman of the IRS to be congenial and completely human, tolerant of my ill-kept records, kind and even humorous. So I prefer to use the better term "publican" instead of tax collector, even though the publican collected taxes. The image of the tax collector in our time needs all the help it can be given, for if it is lawful to pay taxes, it is also lawful to collect them.

Plainly Stated

The lesson of the parable is plainly stated, that whoever advertises personal splendor, his achievements and accomplishments, his civility and charity, his righteousness and rightness is likely to fall flat on his face, while one who hangs his head in self-effacement will be crowned. "Everyone who exalts himself will be humbled, but he who humbles himself will be exalted."

But one can carry it too far, of course, and this isn't always true, although we have a few exhibits we enjoy, especially individuals in whose collapse our own self-righteous indignation found delight. One senses an unholy passion that refuses to let up on Watergate or Chappaquidick or, more recently, on fallen televangelists. Each morning one turns on the news to hear what scandalous event the righteous titillate about today.

The lesson can't be understood without the parable. It is more than mere promotion of humility and condemnation of conceit. "Two men went up into the temple to pray, the one a Pharisee and the other a publican."

This is a bit like saying that in our company at worship, two persons in particular are singled out for notice, one whose presence is no strange experience reserved for smelling evergreens and Easter lilies, but who has a reservation in the same pew every week, and the other, one who slyly sneaks into the back seat of our worship bus, who has not been aboard of late. The first one will be noticed as he leads the aerobics of the liturgy in sitting, standing, kneeling, and in many ways conveys a sense of leadership. If we could see the records, we would probably discover, too, that he is top contributor.

The other is an individual whose name is on the visitation list for special admonition. But no one wanted his name on a list for visitation. No one wanted to assume responsibility for bringing this man back to church or for restoring him to this respectable assembly. Rumor has it that his character is highly questionable, and that although we boast of our inclusiveness, inclusiveness can go too far. Furthermore, they feared that he might blister them a little with a word or two about the righteous pose of this exclusive company, like Mama at the Harper Valley PTA.

What Were They Really Like?

What were they really like, this Pharisee and publican? Would the story ring true in a society today when terms like "righteousness" or "sinner" have been dropped from our vocabulary, when group therapy provides a better outlet from our guilt trips than confession, when dieting is more in style than fasting, and when approval of ourselves and others is more coveted than God's approval?

Both the Pharisee and publican were in the temple as their personal expression of relationship with God, even as we are today. They came to worship, to give thanks, to praise the Lord, just as each one of us has done, I trust. But as we watch them carefully and tune in on their conversation with their God, some differences emerge that tempt our passion for instant analysis.

What happened, for example, to this Pharisee in childhood that he felt the need to list his virtues in the presence of the Lord. Was this the mark of an inferior emotion, an attempt at bold bravado to convince himself, to justify himself? Have we misread him, or is this, in fact, a pride that has been cultivated by so much applause that he believed he was a cut above the rest? Was this hypocrisy, a pious cover-up, or was he actually as blind to need for mercy as he seems?

He was a man who represents what we would like to see in every member of this church. He took religion seriously. He was intent on being a reflection of the glory of God. He would not bring disgrace upon the holy name. He would not be listed on page one among the cheats and chiselers, extortionists and rapists, or in a column on page seven under DUI. He honored the establishment. He obeyed the rules. He was disciplined, his character beyond reproach, and best of all he was a tither. Think of that! What could we do if every member of this church would tithe as he did, not only on his wages, but on all possessions, even dividends and capital gains? We could reach out to the highways and the byways for the lost to bring them in, and we could touch the lives of sufferers whose pain is at our doorstep. We welcome Pharisees as members of the congregation, and might even write a special paragraph in our newsletter as we proudly introduce them to the rest of us. Are we not fortunate to number folks like this among our own?

In his prayer, the Pharisee thanked God for what he was, and if Saint Paul's word had been around, he might have quoted it: "We are God's workmanship, created . . . for good works." He thanks the Lord that he was not as others in the gallery of rogues. And should he not have done so? Should he have denied the good that he had been and hidden his light beneath a bushel? Should he have given the impression that there are no differences between the honest and the cheat, the faithful and the faithless? "God, I have to thank thee." Who else would we thank?

The contrast in the publican is obvious. He represents a fact all too familiar, the obsession of a bad self-image, a total lack of self-esteem. Analysis might suggest that as a child he was controlled at home by guilt, a favorite mechanism of control that parents use. His older brother may have used the put-down to create the atmosphere of inferiority in which he lived and that stayed with him through the years. Perhaps this is the reason why he had sold out to the hated Romans and had become an agent of the enemy. Or was he suffering a depression? Or was his prayer a ruse to cover the bad name that he had gained among his countrymen who saw him as a traitor?

The publican voiced our confession, did he not? "I, a poor, miserable sinner . . ." Is this our genuine self-estimate? Does it honor the God who created us in his own image?

A pastor friend of mine once said to me that when the worship liturgy compels us to the repetition of that statement of confession every week, the people will soon be convinced, and we will have a congregation that is poor, and miserable, and sinful. Was he right?

Who Is a God Like Thee

The story makes it obvious that God is not an analyst, but that he knows our hearts. The ancient prophet Micah, amazed at grace, put it into words like this: "Who is a God like thee pardoning iniquity and passing over transgression?" Would we justify a God who freely pardons, who passes over iniquity, closes his eyes to sin, deals so unjustly with us that he ignores the virtues of the Pharisee and commends the confession of the publican?

Suddenly the focus of the parable shifts from these two

worshipers to the God whose temple they had entered. "Who is a God like thee?" We begin our worship always, not in our own name, but in the name of God the Father, God the Son, and God the Holy Spirit. We cannot saunter down this aisle and take our place before the Lord, tell him who we are and what we have achieved, as though he should enjoy the privilege of our presence. The error of the Pharisee was that he came in his own name, reminding God of lawful obligations that he had fulfilled, behavior which ought to bring God's approbation. To him God might have said, "Indeed! Does that entitle you to something? What do I owe you?" Is there anyone among us who is not familiar with that error?

The error of the Pharisee is that his worship focused on himself. He measured others in the lights of his own righteousness, displayed himself in contrast to the fellow in the rear. "I thank thee, God, that I am not as others are . . . or even as this publican." We call it Pharisaic pride, the easy-but-deadly sin of making odious comparisons between ourselves and others, or, at times, between what we once were and what we now have made of ourselves. Just look at me now! It comes out in gossiping another's failures and in singing the old gossip carol, "Do you hear what I hear?" We are masters of the art.

But the Pharisee and publican, together with us all, stand in the light of God. We are measured by a standard none of us has ever reached. We stand in need of mercy. In the holy Presence Peter cried, "Depart from me. I am a sinful man, O Lord." In the smoking temple of the Lord, Isaiah wept, "Woe is me! For I am lost: for I am a man of unclean lips." And here comes the publican's petition: "God, be merciful to me, a sinner!" As he stood a solitary figure in the presence of his God, the glory was beyond him. Only mercy was within his reach. He, too, admitted who he was, but his credentials were deficient. He took refuge in the Holy Name, the God who comes to us with his credentials, love for the loveless, mercy for the merciless, pardon for iniquity.

Justified

"I tell you, this man went down to his house justified rather than the other."

Why is that word "justified" so difficult? We do it all the time. We justify ourselves, excuse ourselves, defend ourselves, point up our virtues, cover up our faults. We justify the most obtuse behavior, not in others certainly, but in ourselves. We scan the antics of society and say, "That's how it is these days, I guess," but no one ever calls out "Stop it! You are in sin." The unacceptable becomes acceptable as we are conditioned from within and from without to love what God hates, or at best to be indifferent.

God looks us over, but God does not overlook, nor does he wink. God delights in mercy. God forgives. He heals, restores, and reconciles. He justifies. The verdict on the publican is "Justified!" It came not because he used the right words, groveled in the grease, but because in his self-searching he had recognized his need. Mercy!

When we remember who it is who spoke this parable, we learn that these are not mere words. Forgiveness in the Word is forgiveness by an act of God, his act in Jesus Christ on whom God loaded our iniquity, whom he wounded for our transgressions and bruised for our iniquities, and in whose stripes we are healed. The act is Easter and the resurrection when God raised him from the dead and shouted to the world, "Forgiven! Justified!"

In the glitter of our own self-righteousness and in the noise of our achievements, we can blind our eyes and close our ears. Or we can see and hear, and accept forgiveness in his mercy from the hands whose wrists bear the nail prints and the heart that spilled compassion over all the world.

Justified! The old has passed away. All things are new. The unforgiven Pharisee had justified himself, but God ignored the verdict. The Pharisee transferred his guilt to the publican and went home in isolation. But the publican was justified, and went home in joy and newness.

Now talk about self-image! There is none higher. To have one's name inscribed in God's book as a member of his household, to live within the shelter of his mercy, to know that my name has been bound together with the strong name, what more can we ask? To know that he has re-created us in his image, what better image could we covet? God cares for us, and that can only mean that we care, too. God forgives, and, that can only mean that we forgive — forgive ourselves and others. God defends us, and that means that we need not defend ourselves. He justifies in mercy, and that can only mean that there is no more need to justify ourselves in pride. It is a gray and tiring business anyway, trying to downgrade our sin and upgrade our righteousness.

This is old stuff, I realize, and God forgive us, we grow weary of this manna. But for those who bring the sacrifices of a broken heart and contrite spirit, this is new. Mercies new each morning! We have his promise for that.

Luke 19:1-10   *Proper 26 (C)*
Ordinary Time 31 (RC)

The Gospel of the Little Man

Children of all ages quickly recognize Zacchaeus as the little man who shimmied up a sycamore in Jericho to get a glimpse of Jesus as he passed through town. His story has long been a favorite with the children of the church schools, especially those who have experience in climbing trees. His image is imprinted on the mental screen of everyone familiar with the story, for when pilgrims tour the Holy Land and come to Jericho, to see a sycamore rates high in their priorities, and travel guides who find exhibits in the land of Jesus for nearly everything the Bible mentions seldom disappoint them. A sycamore remains in Jericho to satisfy the curious.

But the little man deserves to be remembered for much more than being up a tree. He may have been a little man, small of stature, as the record has it, but he stood tall among the tax collectors in the region. He was the chief publican. He was also in the upper economic echelon of Jericho — very rich. And we remember, too, that on the list of those we love to hate, Zacchaeus held the top spot with his fellow town folk. He had sold out, not only in his compromise with Romans, but to avarice and greed, and his wealth had been accumulated as a traitor to his people. He collected taxes for the hated Romans, adding his own charges to the tax bill. Only when these facets of his character are in perspective does his story slip from the branches of the sycamore and land on us.

The Nub of the Account

The nub of the account is in the stated mission of our Lord: "The Son of man has come to seek and to save the lost," and that's religion talk which many find impossible to understand. Another lesson in the story takes the measure of our penitence as we observe Zacchaeus yielding fruits appropriate to penitence while we have little more to say than "Pardon me, Lord, mea culpa." Or do we find our place among the city folk of Jericho as whisperers of the unrighteous prejudice that blossoms so profusely in the company of self-styled better people, defines the sinner on its own self-righteous terms, and excludes him? They murmured when they saw that Jesus went to be the guest of one who was a sinner, and they were stunned when Jesus said of him, "He also is a son of Abraham."

Recently I read the comments of a man who deals professionally with troubled people. "You see," he wrote, "the church is not for sinners." He explained that it's a place where people come together to affirm their own well-being, not with a sense of guilt, but with a show of righteousness. Listen to the whispered chatter when someone in the company has fallen from their righteous heights. If we think we have no sin, this one is on our record, certainly.

If We Could Have Been There

We wish we might have been there as silent listeners to the conversation when the Savior visited Zacchaeus in his home. We might wish we could have seen the change that in this brief time came over him as Jesus saved the sinner, that we could have read his face when Jesus spoke the word of restoration, or experienced the pathos of his heart when lost Zacchaeus knew he had been found. There is a way we *can* be there. We can understand how small we have become, and come down from our tree now to be confronted by the living Word. Forget Zacchaeus for the moment. The lost whom Jesus seeks and saves have even more familiar names.

Our Story

The Gospel of the Little Man is one that tells our story. It refuses to be left behind in Jericho. It attaches to a desperate need that all of us have known in one way or another — the need, perhaps, created by a desperate outcast feeling, when we have concentrated on our negatives, consigned ourselves to that vast company of little people who are often regarded as of no account. This is not the story of the hot-shot member of the Kingdom from whose up-turned nostrils drip judgments on the little people. It is not the story of a parish godfather whose intention is to make others over in his perfect image. It is not the story of respected righteous people. It is the story of a man who was a sinner, and who in his heart sensed something of his lostness. It is our story. And in a day of shame and self-despising, if our own self-image has grown rusty, we can find new hope in him who seeks and saves the lost.

Little People Count

The story has been told of one of our great choral masters, that one day as he rehearsed his choir, the singers sloughed off on the eighth notes. He stomped hard on the podium, threw his baton against the wall in anger, stopped the choir in its chords, and shouted, "Eighth notes are little people. Pay attention to the little people."

Jesus pays attention to the little people. His mission was to seek and save the lost, the hurting, the despised, the outcast, whether they were always cognizant of being lost or not. He spoke of joy in heaven over one lost sinner who repents, one lost sheep that has been found, one lost coin returned. He spoke the justifying word on one lost sinner in the temple who could only beg for mercy. Here in Jericho he interrupted his procession to Jerusalem, where he would give himself for all the world, to give himself for this one sinner who was lost.

When he comes to us wherever we might be, he calls us by our names: "Zacchaeus, hasten and come down. Today I want to have a talk with you." Can we, then, each one of us, come down, receive him joyfully, and listen to his word of grace?

Personal Salvation

Note, please, that salvation is personal. God so loved the world, indeed, but in Jesus, God gets personal. He is not a God-in-general who rides a chariot in distant regions of the universe, surveying his creation with a loving attitude. Nor does he love the crowd in general, "the community" (as churches like to call it), where each of us can hide and still be swept along somehow. "He's got the whole world in his hands," but he's got you and me, baby, in his hands as well. The best is that he knows us by our names, that he can read our hearts, that he knows our peril, and that he touches each of us personally with his love. We can say he is "our God," and "we believe," but we can also say he is "my God," and "I believe."

If we dare speculate on what that confrontation with Zacchaeus, face to face, involved, I think that it involved a lot of listening. Discipleship begins, not with our talking, but with our listening; not with our words, but with his Word. It certainly involved soul-searching at its deepest level, for however tall this man had stood among his peers or on the economic scene, a sense of smallness in another sense came over him. He was confronted in that visit by the mercy of the Lord in person. He saw and felt a love reach out to him that he had never known or felt before. In the man of Nazareth, Zacchaeus found more than he had anticipated.

No Merchandise

Jesus did not try to sell himself. He never did. He used no evangelistic formula to work conversion. He offered no mini-course in theological dogmatics, conducted no special classes for inquirers, suggested no guidelines for new members in the family of Abraham. He gave this little man the greatest gift that he could give. He gave himself. And this little man, whose tallness in one sense became his smallness in another sense, stood tall again. He was redeemed, restored, forgiven.

We should also add that Zacchaeus did not try to merchandise himself, present a resume of his accomplishments, his past experience, and his impressive references. The resume can be terribly deceiving, as those of us well know who have been stung by self-sales-personship and have hired on a nerd whose only claim to brilliance was the power of deception. Undoubtedly, despite his riches, Zacchaeus never felt poorer, and though small of stature, never felt smaller. But whatever he had sought when he climbed up the sycamore was less than he received before the day was done. He became a walking miracle as he experienced the radical reversal of whatever life had been. More important, he had witnessed in our Lord the miracle that heaven's love had given in the gift sent forth to seek and save the lost. He witnessed Jesus Christ, and in the brief encounter of this hour, he inherited the riches that made all his other riches worthless. He was given stature that no meter stick can measure.

Expectation and Surprise

Whatever prompted this little man to drop his dignity and climb the sycamore we cannot say, except that in his curiosity he sought a passing glimpse of this strange character from Nazareth whose name was on the lips of people everywhere. That he was prompted by a sense of personal need, or by a strong desire in his heart for mercy and a healing of his personal relationship with God and with his fellow citizens in Jericho — this, it seems to me, would push the story much too far. People do strange things and sometimes lose their dignity for lesser reasons, like chasing foul balls in the stadium.

I hardly think this little fellow had a psycho problem, or that he felt a spiritual dilemma, or that his life was up a tree in any other way. But before the sun had set that afternoon, Zacchaeus was surprised beyond the wildest expectation with a healing that he never realized was in his catalogue of need.

Careful! Not Too Close!

Perhaps the story of Zacchaeus illustrates the reason why so many take great care to keep their guard up, hold Jesus at arm's length, when all that they are seeking is a passing glimpse. They will brush against the manger in a Christmas worship. They come to smell the lilies Easter morning. But if he gets too close, or if he suddenly steps forward from the manger or the tomb to visit with us in our homes, those areas of life that we have carefully protected from his interference might be penetrated. Our need for him would then be clear as crystal, and his supply for our deep need a miracle that would upset our every value, attitude, relationship, and corner of our beings.

We recall the parable about a man who planned to build a tower, but who first sat down to estimate the cost. Not a bad idea. When we calculate the cost, we conclude that either we prefer not or we cannot. A rich young ruler came to Jesus with the question, "Tell me what I have to do to gain eternal life." The commandments were old hat, and he had mastered them. He wanted something more significant. But Jesus penetrated through the grease around the question, telling him to sell everything he had and give the proceeds to the poor. The price was too exorbitant. The man was sad, for he was rich. His way to life was blocked.

When we measure stature by the stocks we own, or in terms of our impressive peers, or on the applause meter of public acclaim, when self becomes the center of existence, the cost of being tall in Christ is much too high. The treasure of the living word is worthless in our sight, and life pursues its bitter and relentless course to tragedy. It is simply fact that when our universe is built around ourselves, it cannot get any smaller. Life quickly loses equilibrium and everything becomes disjointed.

"The half of my goods I give to the poor," Zacchaeus said. "And if I have defrauded anyone of anything, I restore it fourfold." It was not as though he questioned it. Fraud had been his lifestyle. His response expressed the fruits appropriate to penitence, not to gain eternal life, but in thanksgiving for the gift he had received.

Specific Salvation

This the Bible calls salvation. For Zacchaeus it meant salvation from the tyranny of things, a total break from the injustice he had practiced all his life, release from seeing town folk as potential customers and objects of his rip-off racket. Greed was transformed to generosity. Guilt was washed away in forgiveness. The barriers were broken down, and he, too, was acknowledged as a son of Abraham.

Salvation means many things in the Bible, but it is always specific, never nebulous. For blind Bartimaeus it meant salvation from his blindness. For the woman taken in adultery it meant freedom from condemnation. For the dying thief it meant the promise of paradise. And when you and I know what we need to be saved from, salvation is real and salvation is the gift of Jesus Christ. From an empty life, from the inner anguish of destroyed relationships, from the grief of loss, from tormenting guilt over those specific sins that clutch our throats, from the bondage of a habit we are powerless to break, from the fear of death — from these we look for salvation, freedom, deliverance. Jesus came to save — save you and me. From what?

Saved For What?

Is there now a warm response to the miracle that Christ has worked for us? Is there a response to demonstrate the miracle that he has worked in us? Those whom we have hurt, offended, lied against, betrayed, oppressed — do they wait in vain for restitution or the simple word, "Forgive me"? The homeless and the hungry, the aging and infirm, the unloved masses that surround us, do they still go begging while we huddle in a cozy enclave with our well-fed friends? The Son of man is come to seek and to save the lost.

Why, then, have *we* come? What is it that gives worth to worthless riches? The worthless riches of Zacchaeus took on worth when they were passed along and used to compensate fourfold those whom he had cheated. And the coins we jingle in the pocket take on worth, the checking-plus account has worth, and even when the Dow is in a dive the stocks increase in value when they support the mission Christ has given us.

Today salvation has come to this house. It has taken hold. Tell me, then, all you little people who have suddenly grown tall in Christ as children of the heavenly Father, what does that mean? Stand tall! Live tall!

John 8:31-36   Reformation Sunday (L)

Emancipation Proclamation

These are slippery words that Jesus used when, fifteen centuries ahead of Martin Luther, nineteen centuries ahead of Abraham Lincoln, he issued the emancipation proclamation: "If you continue in my word, then you are truly my disciples, and you will know the truth, and the truth will make you free."

Slippery words, I said, for when we think we have these concepts, truth and freedom, neatly boxed and wrapped with pretty ribbons, they begin to slip away. The usual baggage we have stuffed inside of them is baggage light enough to handle easily, like carry-ons. We can take it with us in a purse. But on the lips of Jesus they are loaded concepts, heavy (fragile, too), that must be handled with the greatest caution.

But let's burn off the fog. Truth and freedom are not concepts to be clarified or words to be defined. I dare you to define them. In the language of our Lord, they take on flesh and blood. They are personified. They are incarnate in Christ Jesus. "I am the truth," he said, "I am the life." And when you know the truth, the truth will make you free, and freedom, then, takes flesh and blood in you, for "If the Son shall make you free, then *you* are free."

Meet the Truth

Everyone applauds the truth, even chronic liars, but because we have been taken in so often by a claim to truth, we are suspicious of the claim and anyone who makes it. Congressional investigators seek the truth, but after their reports are opened to the public, it depends on your political affiliation, if you have one, whether you accept the truth that their report affirms. "We may never know the truth," we hear it said.

Religious groups make claim to truth, and usually the smaller the religious group, the more exclusive is the claim. We want the truth wrapped up in documents that we can sign our names on as we say, "This I believe." We want the evidence spelled out in terms that cannot be mistaken so that we can say to others in discussion of the truth, "I just can't understand why you refuse to see it." But truth can frequently be found in evidence that seems to contradict the truth.

Courtrooms seek the truth, and every witness summoned to the stand is under oath to tell the truth, the whole truth, and nothing but the truth. Juries weigh the evidence, deliberate, and then announce the verdict. Did they find the truth? Recently my spouse and I sat through the trial of a young man who had been accused of murder. Though he continues to claim innocence, he was convicted by a jury vote of 12 to 0, and recommended for the penalty of death by a vote of 8 to 4. Beyond all reasonable doubt? The defendant was the only black man in the courtroom with an all white jury, prosecutor, public defender, bailiff, court reporter, and a curious audience. We had our doubts about the evidence. We were dismayed by prosecution tactics. One day we may know the truth.

What is Truth?

When Jesus stood before the court of Pontius Pilate, there was an obvious collision of claimed truths. "For this I was born," he said, "and for this I have come into the world, to bear witness to the truth. Every one who is of the truth hears my voice." But the evidence presented by the prosecutors contradicted Jesus, and Pontius Pilate found himself crushed in the collision. "What is truth?" he asked, in what was probably the snide response of one who had been trapped in truths that had been turned and twisted into lies.

Freedom

Add the second concept, freedom. Freedom is the boast of many who have broken down all barriers of restraint. But the broken barriers become the fence of bondage. One does not have to search too far beyond one's own experience for illustrations. Even as we celebrate the Reformation and the contribution Martin Luther made to freedom, we can hear the rattling of the chains. The truth that makes us free is often switched to sidings, while the mainline whistles through our lives, carrying the freight of human answers to the human bondage.

The latest freedom fashion calls for self-expression, to unhook from hang-ups of convention, to be genuine and truly human, but more quickly than we can admit we find that we have only suffered through a change of masters. There is nothing more pathetic than a person who has taken charge of his own life. In his novel, *Texas*, James Michener has Cabeza de Vaca say, "You know, Lad, men are often imprisoned by chains of their own forging." This is not a statement so profound that it escapes our understanding. Each of us has seen it happen — in ourselves, and sometimes in our families, just as the father in the parable had seen it happen to his son, and often in the circle of our friendships. We have felt the icy sweat of hopelessness that comes from finding our feet caught in traps of our own making.

A young lady who is vivid in my memory said she had to take control of her own life. Good thought! There is, indeed, a measure of good sense we have to exercise. But after her divorce, in the midst of problems that divorce creates, she asks, "Who did this to me?" And, of course, she finds an easy answer.

Or is this the answer? "We confess that we are in bondage to sin, and cannot free ourselves."

Did You Say "Bondage"?

This would have been a strange confession for the people in the temple at Jerusalem who had engaged the Galilean in discussion. Crowds had gathered for the feast of tabernacles, and John tells us of a lot of muttering among the people. While some thought he was a good man, others claimed that he was leading them astray. But the muttering was at the level of a whisper, for they feared those who believed in him. In the climax of the dialogue that followed, when they had the opportunity to meet him and to listen to his teaching, Jesus spoke the word that we have named as the emancipation proclamation.

The implication was obvious, and their response immediate, "We have never been in bondage. We are descendents of Abraham. We have the promise." With every Passover, of course, they recalled the bondage of their fathers in the land of Egypt. The Babylonian Captivity was vivid in their history, too. And even at this moment they could not forget that they were being watched by foreigners who occupied their land and that they chafed in their enslavement. But surely they had never lost identity as children of their father Abraham, and "walls do not a prison make, nor iron bars a cage," nor subjection to a foreign power with its occupying army.

But the bondage Jesus spoke of was not physical imprisonment or loss of national identity, but that unrelenting bondage to sin, for "everyone who commits sin is a slave of sin." And sin, as Jesus used the term, did not refer to little naughties here and there, nor even heinous acts of crime, but to a state of slavery.

What we call freedom in our world today is often linked to the political, and conjures up the image of the lady in the harbor with the torch of liberty, or contrariwise, solidarity in Poland, apartheid in South Africa, refuseniks in the Soviet Union, the border guards along the Berlin wall. On the day we worshiped at the Castle Church in Wittenberg, passing through the very door where Luther posted his emancipation proclamation, we spoke with German Christians living in the DDR who in a whisper said, "Wir haben hier kein Freiheit." Yet in the worship hour we had heard an unadulterated Gospel in immaculate German, a description of the freedom that we know in Christ.

What we term freedom in our personal lives is usually the pop-style "freedom to be me," freedom from the prudish customs of our ancestry. Or it might be the plastic freedom after age 16 when we have passed the driver's test, freedom from the watchful eyes of parents. Break loose, express yourself, claim your rights, take control of your own life, and if it feels good, do it — these are the buzz expressions in the whole array of liberation movements. We refuse to be in bondage!

The Liberator

But we confess that we are in bondage to sin, and cannot free ourselves. That's the bad news of the human situation. So when Jesus came to Galilee to preach the Gospel of the kingdom, he launched the greatest liberation movement in the history of the world, a movement never equaled. The Gospel that he brought is God's own emancipation proclamation. It is the Word of Life from him who is the Word of Life, the truth that sets us free in him who is the *Truth*.

Pontius Pilate would have fared much better had he asked not, "*What* is truth?" but "*Who* is truth?" The truth is Jesus Christ who snaps the chains of bondage — our self-insistence, and the guilt that terrorizes us, and the death that would destroy us. The alien power that has occupied our hearts since self-insistence first displayed its wares in Eden has been crushed. Truth is the Christ who loved us and who gave himself for us, who healed the sick, the blind, the deaf, and raised the dead. Truth is the Christ of Calvary who bore in his own body on the tree the lies of all the world. Truth is the Christ who stands before his table as our host and shares with us the broken body and his cleansing blood, "This is *for you*!" Truth is the living, risen Lord beneath whose feet the ultimate, eternal bondage has been shattered and the powers of hell obliterated. Not what, but who?

Liberation — Reformation

The Reformation in the sixteenth century with Luther in the lead role has been credited for many things. It has been blamed for many things. Luther has been praised, and he has been maligned. But at its deepest level, the Reformation was a summons to the Truth, the Truth that makes us free, the Truth who is the Christ. Every word and deed that issued from the church, every teaching commonly accepted as the Truth, even every book of Holy Scripture, was measured in the light of Christ. Luther had no will except to preach and teach the Christ, for in the truth who is the Christ, we are forgiven, justified, redeemed, and freed.

These are great Reformation words, none of which can pass our teeth and lips except for Christ. It is Christ who died for us, and who is raised again for us, in whom we are forgiven. It is Christ who has redeemed a sin-enslaved humanity. It is Christ who has restored us to the highest level of esteem that we can know — children of the heavenly Father.

On this Reformation Sunday, then, we do not mean a tipping of the hat to Luther or to a monument in memory of Calvin, Zwingli, Knox, and all the others. We mean to name the holy name of Truth, Christ Jesus, to know him, to confess him, to experience the freedom and the joy of freedom that he brings. Of monuments we have enough. Of great stone faces in the church we have enough. Of liberated witnesses to Christ, the Truth, we have too few.

On the campus of a seminary I attended just a few years back, there is a Luther statue that I had to pass each morning on the way to class. It was tremendously imposing, this statue of the book-bearer Luther. But often as I passed I wondered why it was neglected, covered with green tarnish, and why the money could not be appropriated to "reform" it every year, at least at Reformation time. It seemed to stand there as a symbol — the symbol of a church grown moldy in neglect of Luther's gospel of the Christ, in the formal recitation of its liturgies, in the busyness of its activities, in pursuit of a religion with no heart. I hoped not.

Reformation Sunday calls us not to reformation, but renewal. It calls us to renewal of a personal relationship with Jesus Christ, not that we can say, "I know what I believe," but this, the more important, "I know *in whom* I have believed." Saint Paul didn't tell us *what* to believe, nor did Luther, nor can I. But on the day I have no witness to the *Truth* in whom we can believe, the *Truth* who makes us free, then on that day the rattling chains will be on audio again, and I will need to know the Truth through you. I trust that you will know him.

We have the promise of our place as free children in the Father's house. Clinging to that promise, we are his disciples, and we will know him, and he will make us free.

Luke 6:20-36 All Saints' Sunday (C)

The Sermon on the Level

The word that Christ our Lord would like to have us hear this All Saints' Sunday is a firm word, gently spoken, lovingly applied. Faintly we recall that he said something similar to this before, in a sermon everyone applauds, but few apply, The Sermon on the Mount.

"Blessed are the poor in spirit," we remember, and we like that. It doesn't touch our assets. "Blessed are those who hunger and thirst for righteousness," and we could use a little righteousness like ours around the nation and the church today. "Blessed are those who mourn for they shall be comforted." It's good to know when the dark clouds roll above us that behind them is a shining sun.

But wait a minute! This word seems to have a different pitch. "Blessed are you poor, for yours is the kingdom of God," and "Woe to you that are rich, for you have received your consolation." Did he mean to say it? "Blessed are you that hunger now, for you shall be satisfied," and "Woe to you that are full now, for you shall hunger." "Blessed are you that weep now, for you shall laugh," and "Woe to you that laugh now, for you shall mourn and weep." Three strikes and you're out, on curve balls low and on the outside corner.

In the version of this sermon that Saint Matthew gives us, it is called The Sermon on the Mount, for when Jesus saw the crowds, he went up onto the mountain, and when he sat down his disciples came to him, and he began his teaching. But in the sermon as Saint Luke remembers it, it can be called The *Sermon on the Level*, for when Jesus came down with his newly-chosen twelve disciples, he stood on a level place and leveled with them on the quality of Kingdom life that was as strange in their time as in ours. It's a quality sometimes admired with awe in those rare folk like Mother Theresa, but as for us in our cash-centered culture, no thanks! A diet can be good for the physique, and fasting can be a spiritual experience, but hunger isn't in our bag of tricks. To mourn will be the lot of everyone occasionally, but there's nothing like a laugh to lift the spirit, and we need a little laughter now, if you don't mind. And then this fourth curve for good measure, "Blessed are you when men hate you, and exclude you, and revile you, and cast out your name as evil." No one on that route will make a sale, and life is lonely without friends.

A Day for Visions

What, then, shall we do with this? All Saints' Day is a day for visions, however strange those visions might appear when measured by the market index, or by the gourmet section of the Thursday morning paper, or by the comic on the tube, or by the applause meter. The vision is the vision of what was, the vision of what might be, and the vision of what shall be. And this last, the vision of what shall be, is the one that hangs us on thin threads of faith as we grow onward in the Spirit, from what was to what can be, before the dawn of glory breaks in all its brightness.

All Saints' Day is the vision of the new Jerusalem, "Coming down out of heaven from God, prepared as a bride adorned for her husband," and the voice from the throne, "Behold, the dwelling of God is with people. He shall dwell with them, and they shall be his people, and God himself will be with them."

All Saints' Day is the vision of that yet more glorious day, "when saints triumphant rise in bright array, and when the King of glory passes on his way."

All Saints' Day reviews the fellowship we have been given,

"the glorious company of the apostles, the noble fellowship of the prophets, the white-robed army of martyrs," and all who fought the good fight to the end, whose company includes all those whose presence we once cherished and whose memory we now honor, who died in faith to live eternally with Christ.

These are visions of faith, of course, visions totally out of touch with the world as we know it, but visions that transform our ordinary days into a great adventure, that bring us together at the table of our Lord with an invisible but mighty host, a multitude no one can number, from all nations, kingdoms, people, tongues.

No Concrete Evidence

But on the level! The evidence suggests that we are far from sainthood. Our style suggests that we might not want to be included in the number when the saints go marching in. There is little that commends such visions to our taste. Between the values and priorities to which we are accustomed and the values and priorities of saints there is a great gulf. In our relationships with neighbors, friends, and enemies, the quality of mercy has been strained, and judgments drop, not like the gentle dew from heaven, but like devastating bombs.

Jesus came to Galilee, preaching the Gospel of the Kingdom, "The time is fulfilled, and the kingdom of God is at hand; repent, and believe in the gospel." The dawn of a new creation was on the horizon. The invasion of the demon empire had begun. As his fame was gossiped across Galilee and into Syria and to the coasts of Tyre and Sidon, many came to hear him and be healed of their diseases, and to touch him as they sense the power that he breathed on them.

But as Jesus leveled with the crowd, he made it clear that Kingdom values were the opposite of every value that humanity has known, and that the Kingdom life, life wholly lived for God in all of our relationships including self, would never be achieved by small adjustments on the screws of life's machine.

In his Sermon on the Level, our Lord describes the life he gives and molds in us as he lays royal claim on us. That life is not achieved. It is a gift. It is not attained by sensitizing people to humanitarian concerns, however noble, or by legislating with another code of laws, or by turning up the pressure with sanctions against the nonconformist. The old creation has to go. The new creation has to come, but it will come his way, not ours.

Confiscated

Life can never be the same. Grace is not a tawdry tinsel on the tree. Discipleship is more than brushing on the Savior's toga sleeve, or tugging at his hemline for a handout. Discipleship is following. It is being claimed by that impelling "Follow me." It is being confiscated and then molded in his image.

So he leveled with them. He always did. Jesus never tried to merchandise himself or sell his cause to unsuspecting prospects. He didn't spend a quarter hour out of every half in an appeal for funds, or advertise a shiny Christmas angel ornament that he would send if you would only write to him. He did not put on a show. He would not accommodate demands of the consumers. He would not be made over in their image. He would make them over in his image.

And here, then, on the level, is the definition and description of his image, the mold in which he presses our hearts now. We are confronted by his Word, not merely tuned in on the Jesus network to be entertained.

Resistance

I can't pretend (I wonder if you can) that I have not resisted. "Blessed are you poor." Does Jesus baptize poverty? Walking Gordon Drive, a street that parallels the Gulf coast here in Naples, as I pass palatial mansions, I ask, "Where was I when all this money was being made?" And I remember where I was.

"Blessed are you that hunger . . . blessed are you that weep." The door that opens widest at my house is the refrigerator door, and if its shelves have not been stocked, there may be weeping and gnashing of teeth.

"Blessed are you when people hate you, and when they exclude you and revile you." I have known that feeling, too, not the blessed one, but the accursed one. The human has a yen for praise, applause, appreciation. Witness how church bulletins list names of persons to be thanked for lifting a little finger for the cause.

Or follow down the list beyond this little paragraph as Jesus drops one jewel on another through the Sermon on the Level. Love your enemies! I thought I heard in your confession that you had not loved your neighbor as you ought. What, then, can you say about your enemies?

"To him who strikes you on the one cheek, turn the other also." No way!

"Give to everyone who begs from you; or of him who takes away your goods do not ask them again." Are there no limits?

"If you lend to those from whom you hope to receive, what credit is that to you? Even sinners lend to sinners, to receive as much again." At 21.9 percent.

A saint in my acquaintance, one of those rare saints who had been blessed with earthly goods, was often touched by people for a loan. A choir member who was less than saintly (as developments affirmed) used him to cosign a bank loan. Not a dime has ever been repaid. The good saint said to me a few years later, "If someone needs some money, I prefer to give it, not to lend it. That route protects the fellow from a guilt conscience when he doesn't pay."

"If you love those who love you, what credit is that to you? . . . and if you do good to those who do good to you, what credit is that?" Another one of my acquaintances who thrives on acclaim numbers a host of friends, but in that number there is not one who questions, contradicts, or criticizes him. Backscratching is a lovely human pastime that pays off.

Touching Tender Places

As Jesus levels with us in this Word, his word is gently spoken, lovingly applied. But it touches tender places, places that have always held high rank with us. In our company today are lovely people who exhibit growth in character and sainthood as the workmanship of Christ and of his Spirit. The soil of their hearts is tilled and cultivated, and the seed that falls there bears fruit an hundredfold. But I have only known one person who could wear this garment — the Son of man who had no place to lay his head, who hungered in the wilderness and at the well of Jacob but forgot his hunger in the mission, and whose tears flowed freely when his good friend Lazarus fell victim to the terror of death, and when Jerusalem chose death instead of life. He promises a trade with us — the garments of the white-robed saints before the throne for the rags of our unrighteousness.

On the level, then. Jesus does not advocate pious poverty to be displayed as holiness. Some of those who are his friends are very rich, as Joseph was, whose tomb became the place for Jesus' burial.

Jesus does not hold up hunger for our adulation. He had compassion on the multitude who followed him into the wilderness with nothing to eat, and he refers the hungry to the care of our compassion. He knows what hunger means, for he identified in his humanity with our humanity. "Give us this day our daily bread" is easily translated by the pleading of emaciated bodies and distended stomachs into "Share with us this day *your* daily bread." Some of us have tender places at the level of the waistline.

Jesus does not require that the faces of the saints wear furrowed frowns or on their arms a mourning band. Joy is their character. One Sunday after worship, a man came out of church and said to me, "Father, I enjoyed your homily." Whereupon he took a sudden elbow in his ribs, delivered by his wife, who said "You're not supposed to enjoy it." But what else are we to do with it if not enjoy it? The purpose of the Word is not to paint the faces of the pious with a sour grimace, but to sound the "tintinnabulation that so musically wells," from the bells of joy.

And certainly the Savior doesn't recommend the idiocy of making enemies with a persistent lack of grace, passing out and all around the acid comments of our moral indignation with a voice of sandpaper.

Priorities are measured here, commitment is confirmed, perspectives are focused. Hearts that are attached to riches of this world, and bottle-popping joys, and carving out a name on granite blocks will print no names on pages in the Book of Life. The poor, the hungry, the burdened, and the scorned are often blessed as favored kingdom heirs, persons whose dependence on the grace of God is heightened in their situation. Not many camels pass through needle eyes. But new life on the level takes the measure of our hearts, not of our bank accounts, and the measure of our minds in Christ, not of our waistlines. And across the Scripture, have you noticed, our relationship with God is frequently defined in terms of our relation to the poor, the hungry, the oppressed. The new life of the kingdom makes the difference.

The Vision of What Will Be

It is quite unlikely that this new life of the Kingdom will stamp its imprint on the lifestyle of the world, that differences between the nations will be settled in a lasting peace, that distrust measured by an arsenal of nuclear advantage will be dissipated, that humanity will gradually progress to its millennium of glory.

But I entertain by faith the vision on this All Saints' Day of what assuredly will be — that by the mercies of the living

God there will be those whose lives are on the altar of God's praise, who will be molded into walking miracles of grace. And in the vision that I share with John, of that great throng before the throne, it may be that I will have to ask, "Lo! Who are these?" But I believe there will be many in that throng whose faces I have seen before and whose names I know, for I trust that you will be among them.

That's on the level. And if you share that vision, too, then I believe the vision of what certainly will be will have a radical and drastic impact on what is now, and we will know that we are in the process of becoming.

Matthew 5:1-12   All Saints' Sunday (L)
                                              All Saints' Day (RC)

Heaven Can't Wait

As we struggle with the burdens of the day, we sometimes wonder, but let the word go forth this morning that we have a future, that however threatening the skies appear, there is no cause for faith to fail. We have the promise of our Lord for that, and he is just as active in our world as he has ever been in anybody's world. He is at work, in a series of unfolding promises, to bring his ultimate promise to fulfillment.

The promise of our Lord is urgent on my heart whenever as a pastor I have opportunity to share the burden of a troubled person, the crisis of decision, the grief of loss, or any of those moments when the future seems to hide behind a wall we cannot penetrate. When counselors, or therapists, or doctors have to say, "This is as far as we can go," or when the sick are terminal, or when a person has to face the end of a disintegrated family and marriage, we have a Word from God that says we go much farther, that there is no wall to separate us from his love, and that the end is in reality a new beginning.

The promise is a greater resource than mere stoic power in the face of trial. God's promise gives a vision of the ultimate which is the blessed assurance that in the present peril, in the hours of our darkness, he is at the helm of life, however anxious, or distraught, or even faithless we may be. He guides our footsteps, faltering though they may be, to the final glory of his Kingdom.

This is the vision that we share together on this All Saints' Sunday — the vision that God shares with us, the vision of a great and glorious future, the vision of our place within that "blest communion, fellowship divine," the vision of that countless throng "from earth's wide bounds, from ocean's farthest coast," streaming in and singing to the Father, Son, and Holy Ghost. What a future!

Heaven is Our Future

Call it heaven, for heaven is our future, friend, the future for us all whose names are written in the Book of Life. That's our future, the new Jerusalem where God is not just something, but where God is everything, where he will dwell with us and we with him, where every tear is dried, where death shall be no more, and where the glory of the Lord, its radiance like a most rare jewel, shall fill the city. That's our future — the day beyond the last check from the government where our security is vested, beyond the coronary, or the cancer, or the hospice, or the other dreadful possibilities. Heaven is our home. "We believe in . . . the resurrection of the body, and the life everlasting."

While those we leave behind cash in our insurance policies, liquidate the assets, sell the house and clear the mortgage, distribute furniture to antique shops, hold a public auction, and divide the spoils, we will have joined another company, those saints of God who served the Lord this side of heaven and who are numbered now in that great cloud of witnesses to grace who have been transferred to the other side. We mean the company of the apostles, the noble fellowship of the prophets, the white-robed army of martyrs, and all the others, too, from our fellowship of friends and loved ones who have died in faith and live in glory. That's the future still to be unveiled for us, the future we behold today in faith, but then by sight. That's the promise toward which all the promises of God unfold, that "As the outcome of your faith you obtain the salvation of your souls."

A Distant Future

In the eyes of many this good word for All Saints' Sunday is a strange word, or if not strange, then something from the distance. One day we might be able to cash in the promise, claim the inheritance, and slip off into something that the Bible and the preacher call eternal life, a blessed relief from pain and peril. For the moment, though, the promise can rest. Heaven can wait.

You know how it is. Even though we realize that life is tentative and that our years are fragile, we live as though we meant to live forever, gathering our toys around us for amusement and amazement, admiring our collectibles, and captivated by the crowds who note our upward mobility and cheer us on to fortune, fame, success, and happiness, or who envy us. We have a passing interest in the many rooms up yonder, but at the moment we are looking for a "5br, 3ba," with a 3-car garage somewhere on the beach at Sanibel. Or life is a ski slope at Jackson Hole. The dessert must wait until we have fully tasted life's main dishes. Heaven can wait.

But the Future is Now

Now shift your mental gears. If that's our future, it's our present also, for the future is in process even now. The future is no longer closed, but open. The Christ in whom we trust destroyed the enemy who slams the door of death against us; Christ devastated his dominion, setting us free from everything that threatens to destroy us. He gave us life and immortality. It took his cross, and then his death, and then his resurrection to restore new life, and the person who believes in him has everlasting life. He has the joy of knowing that his forever is assured and that our freedom from the bondage, each of us in her or his own kind of Egypt, has been won.

Heaven Cannot Wait

But the future cannot wait. If it has opened out the other way beyond the day of our departure, it has opened this way, too. Heaven is at work on us right now. Because it cannot wait for any one of us to shape up to the image of our God in which we are created. The kingdom came from over there to over here in Christ to claim his reign among us now. The foretaste of the future is in Christ in whom we have a new relationship with God, the new creation that the Christ established for us by his cross. The future showed up in the Man of Nazareth who preached good news to the poor, released the captives from their chains and self-constructed prison cells, gave sight to the blind, and life to the dead. The future is at hand whenever in the power of his word the demon empire sways and bends and crumbles. And the kingdom life, so different from accepted lifestyles of the moment, is revealed in his example and his teaching as he drains our mere existence of its common values and re-creates new life in us, new attitudes, new motives, and new values.

Heaven can't wait. That day when Jesus went up on the mountain near Capernaum, sat down with his disciples and instructed them, it was as though he said, "Let me draw a picture for you." And with the master strokes of a verbal brush he painted a new scene that they had never known before. In what is called The Sermon on the Mount, and especially in these verses known as the Beatitudes, he described the kingdom life that he has promised as a gift to all of us, and that he came to bring us through his death and resurrection. This is how we understand the blessedness of that new life described in the Beatitudes — not as a pattern of behavior we achieve by trying harder, by taking charge of our own lives, by a slight adjustment of the carburetor, but the blessedness of life as *he* takes charge and shapes us as his new creation.

The disciples had grown calloused through the years to the usual behavior patterns, the never-ending push for personal progress that uses others as its stepping stones, the eye-for-an-eye and the tooth-for-a-tooth philosophy, the lust for power, passion, and possession. They would often victimize themselves in that same atmosphere, as they elbowed for the seats of honor at the banquet, argued about their comparative greatness, and looked for their own names among the MVP's.

But as they listened to his word, they heard about a life in new dimensions. They knew that there would be some changes made as heaven moved in on them and as Christ began to mold them, not necessarily because they wanted changes, or had it in their power to effect them, but because the Savior had his hand on them. He would work them over, melt them down, and mold them in the image of the kingdom, make them walking illustrations of the reign of God. He would bathe them daily in forgiveness, uproot the pride, the envy, and the spirit of retaliation that infect us all, and so completely overhaul them that their former friends would scarcely recognize them. It would not be easy, but he would make them saints. Heaven could not wait.

The Portrait and the Profile

Watch, then, as the Master paints the portrait and draws the profile of the saints who are to be his workmanship, exhibits what his grace will accomplish in them, and makes the future present in his people.

Blessed are the poor in spirit, for theirs is the kingdom of heaven. Your lifestyle will no longer be determined by what you have or do not have, but by what you are. You have received life as the gift of God.

You will use it in the service of his glory. You will experience the joy of living in his grace without the tiring struggle for a bit of merit. The meaning and the purpose of the poor in spirit is discovered in complete dependency on God without whom life cannot exist.

Blessed are those who mourn, for they shall be comforted. Your lifestyle might demand a never-ending round of party celebrations to commemorate your greatness and your self-sufficiency, but the secret of the life lies in the conscious knowledge that we are not what we ought to be. We have a Savior who supplies our want, beginning with the sin we mourn that cries for his forgiveness. We may mourn the slowness of our progress on the path to sainthood and the ways in which we frustrate his intention for us. A world gone wrong, that shrugs its shoulders with the casual acceptance of the way it is these days, can only search for joy in artificial stimulants, but never know the joy of God's created beauty for our ashes.

Blessed are the meek, for they shall inherit the earth. Your lifestyle might be built on your virility, your drive, and your assertiveness, never realizing how little we have to assert. But the secret of the life of Christ is in that quality appropriate to men and women who are strong in Christ, the courage of consideration, the gentle but strong love in standing for the truth in word and deed.

Blessed are those who hunger and thirst for righteousness for they shall be satisfied. The lifestyle of the world is one of hunger that is never satisfied and thirst that nothing quenches. It's a mad escape from boredom. It's the question, "Are we having fun yet?" But the Kingdom life is newness and refreshment in the mercies of each morning and the opportunities of each new dawn. It's an exciting venture in discipleship, never knowing where the path will lead, but confident of him who leads.

Blessed are the merciful, for they shall obtain mercy. The lifestyle of the world knows little mercy. Justice is in style, a justice that is never perfect even in the best of our humanitarian intentions. The letter of the law is in force. We find glee and gloat when someone fails and falls and when their scandals burst across the headlines, especially if the fallen one has been the object of our hatred or our envy. The character of Kingdom life is in spontaneous expression of the loving heart — giving, serving, reaching for the wounded, compassion for the hurt and bleeding.

Blessed are the pure in spirit, for they shall see God. Our lifestyle seeks pure air, pure water, and pure food, but spurns pure hearts, if not in others, then in ourselves. Acid rain is more a problem than an acid brain. The only god we hope to see is one called me. But the blessedness of Kingdom living is a mind that thinks no evil and a tongue that speaks no evil. When the name of God is on our tongues in prayer and praise, and when the love of God controls our hearts, and when his purity is fastened in our minds, evil has to beat a quick retreat.

Blessed are the peacemakers, for they shall be called the sons of God, the daughters, and the children. We find our favorite game in sowing discord, fomenting strife, and making war, and the paths of life where we have walked are strewn with victims of our weapons, the deadliest of which is that forked tongue between the teeth. The secret of the life is reconciliation, peace, and healing of relationships. It is rooted in the peace that we have found with God who tired of our war against him and who came to Bethlehem in Christ, the Prince of Peace. He shapes us in the image of *shalom*.

We Are His Workmanship

These are the brushstrokes in the portrait and the profile of the saints in whom the future is made present. None of us would claim the portrait and the profile as our own, but heaven can't wait. As Jesus calls us to the kingdom one by one and names us as his own at our baptism, the process is begun. After he has said to each of us, "Your sins are forgiven," the reconstruction work begins. The Beatitudes describe the form, the shape, and the dimensions of the new life he intends to mold in us.

The evidence is here that our Lord is active in our midst, that at least dim outlines have appeared in us of what the future holds in stock for us, and that the outline grows more bold and lifelike daily. As the image of a photograph develops in the darkroom, the image of the saints develops in the light of Christ. You are his workmanship, for in the workshop of his church, as we are shaped by the cutting edges of the Gospel, nurtured at the holy table, the image brightens.

Alone we are as crooked people walking crooked miles and ending up by being hell to one another in a crooked house. But in Christ we have a future that begins to form in us, and we discover what the Master meant, "Blessed are you." Perhaps you can't believe it until you see it. But believe it! Then you will see it!

Luke 20:27-38 Proper 27 (C)
Pentecost 25 (L)
Ordinary Time 32 (RC)

Are There Any Questions?

Today our good year in the company of Dr. Luke, the author of the Gospel that had been in focus through these months, begins to wind down toward the end. Are there any questions? If you have a question, and I suspect we have a few in mind, line up in the center aisle and wait your turn. Jesus has been teaching in the temple at Jerusalem, his disciples are at hand, and in the crowd his enemies as well.

The question-answer period begins. One by one those who oppose him for one reason or another challenge him with questions carefully contrived to trap, expose, and destroy him. The first is posed by scribes and elders and the chief priests of the temple: "Tell us by what authority you do these things, and who gave you that authority."

Next in line are spies who had been sent out by the chief priests and the scribes, who posed their question with a pretense of sincerity: "Teacher, we know that you teach rightly, and show no partiality, but truly teach the way of God. Is it lawful to pay taxes?"

Finally the Sadducees take their turn with a question, one that reflects their point of view as enemies of Jesus: "This woman who had seven husbands, whose wife will she be in the resurrection?"

In every question Jesus knows the deck is stacked, that he is being challenged, and in effect our Lord responds, "Glad you asked that question. It's a good one." In every case the challengers become the victims of their own skullduggery, and some of them are forced to say unwittingly, "Teacher, you have spoken well," and they no longer dare to ask another question.

It is not good educational psychology to crush the questions or questioners, to administer the put-down, to throw wet blankets on the seeking mind. But these tricky questions were not asked by seeking minds, but by unbelieving hearts, not in the search for truth, but as an effort to destroy the truth. As the trap they tried to set for Jesus snapped shut on their own lips, putting them in their place, the more intent they became in putting him in his place — on the cross!

This is not a strange experience. Sometimes in the name of show biz, or for pop entertainment, or now and then in the name of investigative reporting, people of the media hold interviews with an obvious intent: "I'm out to get you."

Now Concerning the Resurrection

The question lifted from the temple teaching of our Lord today is this one, presented by the Sadducees — the question that concerns the resurrection, the highest and most certain hope we have as sons and daughters of the heavenly Father. The Sadducees, we have to understand, did not believe in resurrection, neither Christ's, their own, nor ours. Their question, therefore, was designed to make a farce of it, to present the resurrection in the most absurd and scornful way they could. But we are glad they asked the question, for it lent the opportunity to Christ to underscore again this platform of our faith, to set an Easter fire glowing.

> *There came to him some Sadducees, those who say there is no resurrection, and they asked the question, saying, "Teacher, Moses wrote for us [back in the Book of Deuteronomy,] that if a man should die without a child, it is his brother's duty to take his wife and provide an heir for him. Tell us, then, there were these seven brothers, each of*

whom in turn fulfilled his duty as another brother died without a child. In the resurrection, whose wife will the woman be, for each of the seven had her as his wife."

Luke 20:27-33 (Paraphrased)

It was a question filled with interesting implications for the curious, the sort of question prurient interests love to dwell on, and it was certain to attract the audience. But sweeping all those implications out the door, "I'm glad you asked that question." Even though it had been asked in ridicule, it sets the scene in which to challenge our priorities in life, that myopia which only sees the present moment. It challenges our hopes, our goals, and all the passions that consume us, the direction that our lives are taking, and our vision of the kingdom.

The Ultimate in Faith

It is the ultimate in Christian faith that we are heirs to a great fortune put in trust for us, that we are children of the resurrection, that the God of Abraham, the God of Isaac, and the God of Jacob is not a God of those who have been buried in the graveyard, dead and gone forever, but a God whose children are alive and well. It is the ultimate in Christian hope that our inheritance is incorruptible and undefiled, reserved for us where thief cannot break through and steal, nor rust corrupt, nor moth destroy. We have his promise. We anticipate the victory of the resurrection in the coming of the Christ who in his first appearing died for us and rose again, and promised that because he lives, we, too, shall live. In that victory we have the ultimate in Christian joy, a bliss no way inferior to that of holy angels in the presence of the Lamb. The Lamb of God, who took away the sin of world, who washed us in his blood and made us worthy to be counted as the sons and daughters of the Kingdom; the Lamb of God, who in his dying on the cross bore all the guilt of all humanity (no way can we begin to comprehend it), this Lamb brought the peace no fear can smother, the joy that has no equal. We heard it at the Easter tomb where angels first proclaimed it. We watched the Lord's apostles as they carried it around the world, the only message that they knew: "He was offered up for our sins; he was raised again for our salvation." We saw it spread from continent to continent, as dying men and women reached from helplessness for heaven's help, from hopelessness to living hope. And it became our own when our old sinful nature drowned in the water of baptism and we were given the risen and new life in Christ.

Christ has died! Christ is risen! Christ will come again! The news is so astounding, the impact so emotional, that we cannot restrain ourselves. As the Great Thanksgiving of the Eucharistic prayer is spoken, we interrupt with loud exclamation, "Christ has died! Christ is risen! Christ will come again!" Could that exclamation tolerate a sleepy mumble from the Sunday saints before whose eyes appears the vision of the great white host before the throne of God, who are about to know the greatest privilege this side of heaven in the banquet of grace? With hearts fixed on his exalted throne from which he condescends to be with us in mercy, life has to bounce with joy.

When all is said and done, when everything we lived for, planned for, worked for, hoped for has been taken from us, when torn hearts spill their grief at graveside, the promise heals. "In my Father's house are many rooms. I go to prepare a place for you . . . and I will come again, and I will take you to myself." And in the not-so-distant future, faith can hear the resurrection trumpet sound. The human scene of decay and death and broken hopes and evaporated dreams fades out, and this bright vision comes in focus, "Behold, I make all things new."

Do You Have a Question?

I suspect that there are many questions, any one of which, if asked sincerely and in truth, would find an understanding heart in Christ. When our physician recommends a surgical procedure for an illness, we have many questions. What are the percentages? How long will I be out of business? What can I expect beyond the surgery and time of convalescence? Of course, what are the charges? But even after all the questions we can think of have been answered, there will be a few surprises. And remember, please, there are no guarantees.

When our financial counselor advises an investment in a mutual fund or in a stock or in municipals, we have questions. What are the percentages? Is this a growth fund or an income fund? What kind of history does the fund recite? But remember, please, there are no guarantees, regardless of how much in your interest your counselor appears to be.

When the travel agent recommends a cruise, we have questions. What does the price include? Inside or outside cabin? How many ports of call along the way? Has the ship's food service been approved by health inspectors? There are no guarantees that every detail will be delightful, that the sea will be calm, or that the ice cubes in the fruit juice when you come ashore in Cartegena will be pure. Montezuma's revenge can be frightful, I have learned.

And since we know in certainty that heaven is our home, the resurrection victory is in sight, death has been defeated, everlasting life awaits us, we have questions. While there will be surprises in that heaven, this certainty is guaranteed. But the most important question we can ask today is this one: "Does it make a difference? How can we show the difference?"

This was the question that a young man asked who in his third college year, while home for Christmas, came again to visit with me. In previous visits he had always brought on his heart the turmoil, the confusion, and the doubt his questions reflected, and often while away at college, he would write long letters that expressed the same. This time as he came in, he couldn't wait to get it out: "I have found perfect peace!" And when I must have looked surprised, he blurted out, "I am now an atheist."

"Tell me about that," I responded.

And he told me. He told me of the dogma he had tried to swallow in his younger years that had been fed to him by parents, and, of course, by me, his pastor. "I choked on it," he said, "and had to use a kind of Heimlich method to pop it from my throat."

He added that in Christians he had known, he heard a lot about the difference their faith made, but never saw it. He cited those knock-em-down-and-drag-em-out encounters that the church (our parish, too) has had where people choose up sides and fire rockets at each other. He recalled a series of false accusations made against the pastor by a clique of dissidents who held secret meetings and were out to get him. He intended that his life was going to make a difference, that he would work for justice, truth, morality, equality, bread for the hungry, and above all, just plain honesty.

He was right, of course, and there could be no argument. Christian values are sometimes more in vogue with atheists than Christians. The only new life he could understand was the new life he intended to create.

His ideals were high, his goals were noble. And his assessment of the little difference that the faith reflects in many could not be contradicted. But I have followed his career with interest, and after a long series of distresses, he is in the fold again — not in my church, but in another. And strangely, it is where the dogma is thick and where the battles rage in public view. His idealisim has been replaced with realism, but I want you to know that this young gentleman today is one solid witness to the difference that the resurrection faith has made in him. He was gone, but he is found.

The Resurrection Life is Now

What difference does it make? The resurrection life is not a deli in the sky where we can purchase our dessert when life's main course is finished. The resurrection life is *now*, life lived not for ourselves, but for the God who loved us long before the world was made, who redeemed us at the price of blood, and who has given us new birth. That changes everything in life — the way we run our business, the way we play the game, the language that we use, the way we deal with our oppressors, the way we make investments. It frees us from the chains of our own forging. It removes the handcuffs of our fears, self-centeredness, and selfishness — to touch the leper and the sin-stained and the burdened.

In my first year as a pastor, on one of my first nights in western Canada, I mistakenly tried driving home along a section road. It was just long enough beyond a rain so that the soil had become a sticky mud. After only a few yards, the mud had rolled and balled around the wheels, preventing further progress. There was no way out except to walk. But this soil that grows the finest wheat crops in the world is known as gumbo, and the gumbo sticks and builds and balls around the feet until one's legs become so heavy that one can hardly move.

I find this a picture of the way our lives are often lived, feet glued to the gumbo, the weight of things, concerns, and interests that stall our spiritual growth. We pan for our share of the gold, pile up reserves for our security, make friends with those who can promote our cause, until the gumbo threatens to glue us to the grave.

The hope-filled Word is this: "I am come that they may have life and have it abundantly." An abundant life, he said, not necessarily abundance in life, for the abundance can easily become the mud, our possessions the possessor, and ourselves the possessed.

God of the Living

God is not a God of the dead, but of the living, and the children of the resurrection live to God. The glow of eternity is in their hearts. The Christ who has prepared a home for us is the guiding light. Does that make a difference?

Glad you asked that question. Now let's *see* your answer.

Luke 21:5-19 *Proper 28 (C)*
Pentecost 26 (L)
Ordinary Time 33 (RC)

How to Stay on Top of It

Memories of my father are as vivid in my heart and mind today, thirty years beyond his going home, as on the day those memories were in the making. Mother is included, too, but for my purpose here, I mention Dad especially. To my youthful mind he always seemed to be on top of it. He was down to earth, lived in the midst of life's realities, and never soared on clouds with spiritual fanaticism. The gospel according to Dad included frequent trips with us to Green Bay Packer football games and Milwaukee Brewer baseball games, batting fly balls to the boys (he was denied the special privilege of girls) out on his rural church lawn, soft-spoken but incisive comments on world news events, gardening and chicken farming on the parsonage acreage, and foremost a faithful pastor's ministry.

Frequently across the years of memory I have recalled the line he often wrote in letters to our family after we had gone from home: "Our chronic weakness is not that we expect too much from God, but that we trust him for too little." Or when the rural parish that he served could not be isolated any longer from the jitters of our time, his comments would include, as he described reactions he had seen to fearful incidents, "Where is that calm confidence that underneath are the everlasting arms?" He was a patient man, especially patient with his sons, seldom agitated, seldom stressed. No matter what would happen, he seemed to know that everything would be all right.

In fact, the only times I can recall his agitation came when listening to a Packer-Bear game, when the margin narrowed and he was not sure that everything would be all right. Except for that, he always seemed to be on top of it, for God would have the final word, not in football, but in history and in life.

The virtue of his patience is not one that I inherited. Sometimes I recall him telling me, "Don't swat at flies with a baseball bat." Frequently he shared the secret of his patience, something about drawing strength from the certainty of God's promise, but I have had to work at that, and have not even now attained. It has to do with faith, and trust, and hope, and how to stay on top of it.

Life With Its Ups and Downs

In this frenetic century, which has always seemed to be on the edge of a nervous breakdown, the sense of being on top of it needs careful cultivation. I suspect that there are many like myself who have a problem here, for statistics on this ulcered, hypertensive generation seem to bear out that suspicion. Children of the heavenly Father are bombarded in this anxious age as everybody is. We are caught up in the tensions and the stresses life imposes, and the prospect of the third millennium ahead for those who can endure that long are not as bright as prophets with rose-colored glasses might propose. The unprecedented pace of progress will quicken even more, but the brave new world continues to be threatened by an endless list of hideous possibilities. Our security has never been more insecure. Friendships have never been more tenuous. Vaunted progress has never been more tested. The highs of our drug culture have become the lows of desperation. When we reach the top in one sense, we are at the bottom in another. To say life has its ups and downs is much too mild.

Approaching the End

The clock ticks down now on another year of grace, and Jesus has a word to say to us about the future just ahead and the future in the long haul. It is not a pretty picture that he paints. He doesn't share the hope of politicians who promise us a golden age of glory, a great society, a generation of peace, a world of social justice with respect for human rights. The torch that was "passed to a generation born in this century" has not been burning with strong flame. Nor does our Lord have much confidence in the efforts of church politicians who envision a bright future for the Kingdom in this world, who prattle with a be-happy gospel, especially not if we confuse our little kingdoms with his Kingdom. He has a better word on how to stay on top of it. It is this, that when everything is dark and there is no flickering match at the end of the tunnel, look up through the darkness, raise your heads, fear not, for "I have overcome the world." "Not a hair of your head will perish." "By your endurance you will gain your lives." The final chapter, the final page, the final paragraph is certain. The outcome is sure. Wait. Wait patiently! We have his promise.

Disaster Ahead

That's the word in this great chapter from Saint Luke. Our Lord was in the temple at Jerusalem, just a few days from the Cross. Although this temple ran a distant second to the glory of the temple that was Solomon's, this was a beauty, too, almost enough to rival the cathedrals that have been the symbols of the Christian glory since — Saint Paul's in London, the Duomo in Milan, Saint Patrick's in New York, the Crystal Cathedral in Garden Grove, or even that magnificent new edifice that Pastor Jones' church built on Prosperity Avenue to make a name for itself. Jesus heard the comments of the curious tourists in the crowd, expressing wonder at the beauty of the stones for which the lowly widow had contributed her offering, and Jesus said, "As for these things which you see, the day will come when there will not be left here one stone upon another that will not be thrown down."

It had to shake his followers! That this temple where they sought the presence of the living God would be destroyed, this place that was the bulwark of the Hebrew faith, or these attractive churches that we build, the impressive organized religion we are proud of, the budgets we raise and the numbers we gather in with our crusades — that all of this goes down the pipes, has to shake his followers. These are the measuring tools of our effectiveness.

But it seems that his disciples were not shaken in the least. The immanent disaster that they faced, the devastation of the temple that had been their pride, the complete destruction of the holy city, nothing seemed to shake them greatly. "When will this be?" they asked, "And what will be the sign when this is about to take place?" Their question indicated that they looked for this event to herald the arrival of the Messiah and the Messianic age, the fulfillment of their hopes and longings, the golden age, the great society, the brave new world of social justice, apartheid ended, terrorism finished, inflation at point zero, interest rates below the usury level, an economic boom without the bust, a bullish market, AIDS cured and cancer conquered, no more nukes.

The coming of the Messiah was and still remains the hope of Israel. Pilgrims to Jerusalem will notice in the eastern wall the Golden Gate through which, it is suggested, the Messiah will arrive. The gate was blocked by Sultan Suleiman, as the story goes, to insure that no messiah would ever come through that gate. But Christians, too, with the Apostle Paul have turned their eyes to that decisive day when the kingdom in its fulness will break through and be revealed, and when history ends at the Messiah's throne. Our fervent prayer, "Thy kingdom come," reflects the hope that has ever been the church's secret strength, the assurance of the promised victory of God.

From that perspective, knowing what the final outcome of our history will be, we live and do our mission now with confidence, always on top of it. We can live with heads and hearts uplifted, not with confidence in human progress, but because in Christ the old has passed away and in the tiny mustard seed the hidden kingdom of our Lord is on the way.

The Hopeless, the Hoping, and the Hopeful

Recently I heard the differences described between the hopeless, the hoping, and the hopeful. The hopeless folk have given up on life and God, and have become despairing, negative, and cynical. The hoping folk are looking for some sign of hope, reading messages in fortune cookies, studying their horoscope, buying tickets at the lottery, and meanwhile watching out for black cats on their pathway. But the hopeful are the people who can see God's end and new beginnings in his promise.

The Warning

Jesus did not answer the disciples' question. Instead he issued a broad warning about false messiahs who would claim the office of messiah, saying, "I am he. The time is at hand." Do not be led astray. And instead of giving them a sign as they had asked, he said that in the latter days there would be tragedies and wars, and while this often has been understood to mean that judgment and the end were on the immediate horizon, he added, "But the end will not be at once." Nation against nation, war and tumult, earthquake, famine, pestilence — these are bold reminders that the world will not go on forever, that the fulness and the revelation of the kingdom is certain, but that his coming in the day of victory will not be fixed amid our end-time fireworks.

There Will Be Work to Do

First, there will be work to do. Luke in his evangel says it this way, that "the gospel must first be preached to all nations." That's our in-the-meantime business, and we are to be perpetually on top of it. It will not be easy, for if the Master traveled pathways of rejection to the Cross, can his followers expect a better road? "They will lay their hands on you," he said, "and persecute you, delivering you up to the synagogues and prisons, dragged before kings and emperors and governors for my name's sake." We may be subjected in our time not so much to persecution as to scorn, or simply being ignored, or if persecution, it might be more likely from within than from without. But this will be a time for testimony, not a time to retreat into a holding pattern. It will be a time for witness, not for speculation on the where, the when, the how.

Our work, if one may call it work, is to proclaim the Gospel of the Kingdom, the Christ who was delivered for our offenses and raised again for our salvation. "Repent and believe the gospel . . . The kingdom is at hand . . . For God so loved the world . . . Your sins are forgiven . . . Christ brought life and immortality to light . . . Because I live, you, too, shall live." The Gospel of the Kingdom is our message. Wait! Wait, I say, on the Lord.

But I mean active waiting. A recent journal published by a national church body carried a full-page commentary on the mission of that church beneath the headline *Lutheran Evangelism is a Joke.* You can be certain that this commentary flushed out several dozen letters to the editor. It might have been Episcopalian or Methodist or Presbyterian or any of the mainline structures which hide wholesale losses behind religious hype while they preserve their proper Presbyterian procedures, their Episcopal succession, or their Lutheran orthodoxy — in general, their good company. The truth is bolder than fiction. We have not been on top of it.

This is a time for testimony to the Cross and Resurrection,

and the final victory of Christ. In a recent Easter Sunday worship, fifteen minutes into a sleepy moral essay on love, I distracted my spouse by writing on the service folder, "I thought this was Easter. Do I have the wrong day?" The resurrection Word had been silenced. There was no Eucharist to save the day. But there were lilies in the chancel.

Testimony — the resurrection Gospel certainly, but also testimony through our Spirit-led demeanor. That calm confidence that underneath are the everlasting arms is not possible without the resurrection Gospel, but in the resurrection Word is power that preserves us from the shakes and shivers of the day. The assurance that endurance will secure our lives enables us to stay on top of it and live above the perils of the present even though we live within them. The promise of his triumph in the end and in his purpose also makes us masters of the situation now and people full of hope, so full that it spills over in a faithful witness. We do not play with cards that have been dealt to us, as people say with gritting teeth, clenched fist, and growling stomach. We are working with the love of God that has been given us and that enables us, even when the mountains threaten to fall over on us.

We have his promise, the promise sealed because the tomb's seal was broken. In the impatience I did not inherit from my father, I need that promise, and that ought to be enough, even for me.

Luke 19:11-27   Pentecost 27 (L)

Advancers Over Decliners

The parable of Jesus that Luke shares with us today does not rate highly in the polls. If, indeed, we did a survey among Christians with regard to parables, not only favorite ones, but parables in general, it is likely that this story would be missing from the list entirely. With slight variations, it appears in Matthew and in Luke, in Matthew as the Parable of the Talents and in Luke as the Parable of the Pounds, but while each writer has his own unique elaborations, in substance both of them are writing the same story.

But this one does not occupy a cherished place within the hearts of most of us as other parables of Jesus do. This one can't be sentimentalized as we have often sentimentalized the favorite and familiar. This one can't be sweetened with a little sugar from the bowl of pop-style religion. It doesn't throw us into the welcoming arms of God as though he were our heavenly babysitter. When we sweep aside the cobwebs of confusion that are spun by spiders in the mind around so much of Holy Scripture, this one speaks directly, bluntly, even harshly as it lays its warning on our hearts.

Let's get to it, then, for as another year of celebrating grace in Jesus Christ winds down, this parable can serve as prelude to the wrap-up, not only of another year, but also to the wrap-up of world history, or more pointedly, our personal histories. "When the nobleman returned, having received the kingdom, he commanded his servants to be brought to him, that he might know what they had gained by trading." The day of reckoning had come. Give an account of your stewardship.

The final Dow, with a summary of advancers and decliners, was to be given.

The Purpose of the Parable

Luke tells us that the parable was spoken to disciples who anticipated that the kingdom of God was to appear immediately. As they left Jericho, where Zacchaeus had received salvation, they continued upward on their journey from the Jordan Valley to Jerusalem where they expected Jesus to assert himself, claim the Kingdom, usher in a new world order, take his power and reign. Indeed, Jerusalem would be the site in which his kingly rule would be established, but not as they anticipated. His kingly throne would be a cross, his crown a crown of thorns, his homage the raucous cries, "Crucify him!"

With this stated purpose of the parable, the story hardly seems to fit our crowd today, for there are few of us who entertain the dream that those disciples entertained. Perhaps we envision a better future for our world when human sensitivities are sharpened and the human race becomes more lovable and loving, when an arms-control agreement reduces the threat of nuclear annihilation, when a cure for AIDS, Alzheimer's, diabetes, porosis, or even the ancient common cold is found. But experience has taught us not to hold our breath. And as to that great creedal statement, that he will come again in glory — few of us expect the Kingdom to appear within a day or two. I have heard folks ask it many times, "What is this world coming to? Where will it end?" Sometimes I have heard the plaintive chant, "The answer, my friend, is blowin' in the wind." Except for a burst of optimism here and there, we pursue our course one day at a time, make personal plans without consideration for the will of God, Deo volente, and for a break from life's routine we stop to smell the roses now and then and prick our thumbs on thorns. As for the Kingdom of God, we have been enroute in that direction for 2000 years, but there is little sign of its appearance.

But the Purpose Has a Point

A certain nobleman, the story tells us, called his servants to a meeting, announced that he was leaving for a distant country to receive a kingdom, entrusted to each one of them a pound, then left with no return date set. At his ultimate return, he called his servants in for an accounting. Two were able to report advances in the value of his stock, and both of them received warm commendation for their faithful stewardship. A third confessed that he had been afraid to risk his pound, that he had laid it away in a napkin, or hidden it beneath his mattress, or buried it in a tin can in his back yard, or put it in a bowl on the top shelf of the pantry. Without allowing for inflation, he could now return it to the master at full value. And it's obvious that he expected to be complimented for his cautious care and honesty.

Instead, however, this extreme conservative, as we might call him, was rebuked in no uncertain terms. "You wicked servant, I will condemn you out of your own mouth. You knew that I was a severe man . . . why then did you not put my money in the bank, and at my coming I should have collected it with interest?" Then came the judgment: "Take the pound from him, and give it to him who has the ten pounds . . . to everyone who has will more be given; but from him who has not, even what he has will be taken away."

The first servant was commended, "Well done, good servant! Because you have been faithful in a very little, you shall have authority over ten cities," and your faithfulness will be entrusted with much more. The second servant, too, received his commendation in the form of an assignment over five cities. But the pound entrusted to the third was taken from his care and given to the faithful one. If he could not be faithful with a single pound, could he be given more responsibility?

It should be said that Jesus in this parable does not intend to lend support to our Wall Street syndrome, investments in the market, or the growth funds recommended by our broker.

But in today's economy with all its complications, the ups and downs of bonds and stocks and bank certificates, the interest rate, inflation, and tax structures, good stewardship requires just a little more of savvy than a tin can buried in the yard.

Nor does the story advocate an economic policy whereby the rich get richer, and the poor become poorer, as the parable appears to say, "to everyone who has will more be given; but from him who has not, even what he has will be taken from him." And certainly the parable does not support the growing fiction spread by those who merchandise religion that when you give your heart to the Lord you will be blessed with higher profits, better business. "Try this wonderful new product," the religion hucksters tell us, "Jesus!" And the promise is that he will make you feel good, even help you get rich quick.

The Point is This

The point is this. To each of us in equal measure has been given that most intimate relationship with God as children of his family. Through Jesus Christ, his Son, he loves so much that he went straight to Calvary to die for us. He was willing in his love to take our chains of guilt on his own hands and feet and let them bind him to the cross. He wore the crown of thorns and suffered scorn from those who had refused and still refuse to have him as their king. With such love he has drawn us to himself and laid his claim on us as his redeemed. We are his children now. We are his servants. From aimless wandering without a goal beyond the grave, from our self-centered ways that know no business but our own, and from the poverty of nothingness he has delivered us and given us a place in which to serve with noble and enduring purpose, and inherit LIFE — in capitals!

This is our pound, given each of us in equal measure. Gifts and talents have been given us in differing measures but in this important gift there are no advantages or disadvantages one has that others do not have. Each of us received the pound when God took us to himself in Holy Baptism, washed us in the cleansing blood of Christ, locked his promise on our hearts. You heard that right: we all receive in equal measure, none loved less than others, none loved more than others. "Trade with this," the Master tells us, "until I come."

But the decliners outnumbered the advancers. What happened to the other seven servants in the parable we are not told, but there were citizens who sent an embassy to tell the nobleman that they would not accept his rule. They would be gainers, go their own way, do their own thing. The lordship of our lives is never easily surrendered. Enslaved by sin and trapped by self, life is reserved as our domain, no interference tolerated. But there is nothing more disastrous to be heard from human lips than this, that "I intend to take control of my own life." In the end, at Christ's return, there will be no need as in the parable to summon those who had refused his rule to be destroyed. Self-destruction has already been a fact. Contemporary forms of bondage are in evidence aplenty, and the living hell to which they lead us is the deadly, sad experience for throngs. Decliners far outnumber advancers.

Is it probable that we might see our portrait painted, not in those who would refuse the Savior's rule, but in that third servant with his pound wrapped up in Kleenex? Religion is a personal thing, we say, something deep within our hearts. We box it up in our devotions, or in Sunday liturgies, or we chain it to the altar of our churches. We are children of the heavenly Father when we "safely in his bosom gather," but beyond the doors of our stained-glass cathedrals that good feeling might evaporate. Out here in the world the pound could easily be lost. Therefore, let there be no risk. Walk the straight and narrow, do what is right, obey the rules, let piety parade in worship, but then stuff it all inside the pocket of the soul and carefully preserve it.

Remember, too, how often we suppose that with our little pound so little can be done. To light a candle in our corner of the world would make no difference anyway, and ill winds that blow across the nations with the force of hurricanes would surely blow it out. "If I had a lot of money," someone says, "or if I were a gifted and important person in the power structures, then I could . . ." Could what? The question is not whether we would be more faithful (given riches, power, and position), but whether we are faithful with the pound we have. The spiritual capacity we have been given will enlarge as it is used. It will be lost if never used. And how frequently does it not happen that the distance from the font to the pig sty is traversed by a hoarded or inactive faith? Are we in a bearish market? Decliners outnumber advancers?

Use Your Gift

Use your gift. Be faithful to your trust. Trade with this until I come. Here in our company of faith, I trust that advancers will outnumber decliners, that each of us will take the pound we have been given and employ it and invest it as his servant. John Powell, an author and a Roman Catholic priest of popular renown, has hanging on his bathroom mirror a sign that he will see each morning as the first thing on the day's agenda. "Good morning, Jesus! Thank you for loving me. What have you got going today? I want to be part of it." At a church that I attended recently, the pastor had prepared a copy of that sign for everyone at worship to take home. I put it on my mirror, too. But I confess that often with my mind preoccupied with daily business of my own, I failed to see the sign, or seeing it, I wished I hadn't. Yet I believe that every day is given as an opportunity to exercise the spiritual capacity I have been given, to be a part of God's plan in the world, and that whatever plan I have ought never contradict his plan. Each day is an investment in his love, for every day belongs to him and is in trust to me. Then we can move out through the garbage that piles deeply on the paths of life — anxieties, reverses, tragedies — or if not the garbage, then the happy things he gives in such abundance, and we can know that taking Jesus at his promise, we can risk, invest, and work for him. The top line in discipleship, never the bottom line, is taking seriously our relationship with him, at least as seriously as he took his relationship with us. He died for that. A risk on our part is appropriate.

That may mean saying to a neighbor with a bleeding heart, "Come, let me share it with you. I know a Lord who heals." Or it may mean saying, "The pathway you are taking, what you are doing, is wrong! Stop it. Stop it now. I know a Savior who can get things turned around." It may mean saying to the members of your comfortable and cozy fellowship at church, "We are not here to preserve the faith. We can preserve it only when we share it." It may mean many things, but as faith grows and responsibility and trust increases, the opportunities for your investment and your risk will pop up everywhere. Well done, good servant.

Luke 23:35-43   *Christ the King (L, RC)*

Believing is Seeing

When Jesus came to Galilee, he began his preaching with the message, "Repent, for the kingdom of heaven is at hand." And the expectations of the people soared to heights not known since Solomon. They had been oppressed, depressed, distressed, and had been waiting for the day when from their midst a hero would arise to lay a left hook on the jaw of the hated Roman Empire, restore the glory of the dim and distant yesteryear, and make those good things happen that the prophets had foretold. The land should bloom again, poverty should be exchanged for prosperity, and swords should be beaten into plowshares.

So there were fishermen who dropped their nets and followed him. There were zealots who became excited at the prospect of the kingdom, a tax collector closed his booth and invested his stock in this new opportunity. People brought their sick to him, the pained, the paralytic, and the infirm, for as he preached the gospel of the kingdom, he healed them of their diseases, and cast out demons. His fame spread southward to Jerusalem and north to Syria. The skies were bright with promise.

We can understand the mood. We have heard the promise that prosperity is just around the corner. We have heard the bands strike up the tune, "Happy Days Are Here Again." We have been given the assurance of a great society, a generation of peace, and the great things that should happen because the torch was passed to a generation born in this century. We scan the headlines, watching for the breakthrough that might promise cures for our diseases, aches, and pains. We cheer the tax reform that promises more disposable income. As someone once or twice was known to say, "Progress is our most important product," and we are on the move.

But as our expectations soar, disappointment deepens. Visions of the Kingdom evaporate. Ideals dampen to realities. The mood of the Emmaus disciples takes hold again. "We had hoped . . ."

What, then, shall we say to this — this sudden burst of pyrotechnics as the church on this last Sunday of the church year, the day of Christ the King, brings in the royal diadem to crown him Lord of all? Is this another round of hype and hoopla? Do we crown what seems to be our last-place finish with a "Wait Till Next Year" banner in our bleachers? Patience wears thin on coaches who defend their losing season with the promise that we are building for the future. To say that *Christ is King*, isn't that like saying that the cellar is the ceiling? If Christ is King, then . . . and each of us can name his own demands and voice his own objections that in one way or another ask for evidence and proof. "Show me! I'll believe it when I see it."

Believe It, Then You'll See It

But flip the coin. "When I believe it, then I'll see it." For the word that crowns him Lord of all intends that all of us should see it, not by sight, but by faith, for faith is the assurance of things hoped for and the conviction of things not seen. And we will never see it until we believe it. The thief who dies at Jesus' side would never recognize him as the king by looking at him with his eyeballs only. But when he believed, then he saw.

Contrary evidence has always been in rich supply, and this was no exception as Jerusalem observed an execution day. None of us would dare confuse an execution with a coronation. By nine o'clock that Friday morning Pontius Pilate, against his better knowledge, had agreed to the demands that had him backed into a corner, and our Lord was on the cross. The death march from the judgment court to Golgotha, a journey that has since been cherished by all Christians as the Via Dolorosa, had reached its goal and Christ was crucified.

The Signs of Royalty

There were few signs of royalty. Herod had contributed a purple robe as he returned the prisoner to Pilate for the final judgment. He wore a kingly crown of thorn, and overhead at Calvary there was the royal superscription JESUS NAZARENUS REX IUDAEORUM. Whether it was meant by Pilate as mockery of Christ or as mockery of those who sought his death is not completely clear. He did not intend it, certainly, as his confession of the faith. One could also hear, from those participating in the scene, satanic scorn for all suggestions of his kingship. There were no kingly tributes. "If you are the king, save yourself." "We have no king but Caesar."

It Had Come to This

So this is what the Gospel of the Kingdom now had come to. Here those heightened expectations crashed. Talk about those kingdoms on the rise and wane. None ever rose and waned like this one! And even those professed disciples of the Kingdom, except for one who stood compassionately at the side of mother Mary, had lambed out. By three o'clock that afternoon the imposter king was dead. The world had heard the last of him. The pits of Hades must have echoed with the noise of celebration that could rival any victory blasts in locker rooms of champions. The best that could be done was done by Joseph of Aramathea, a good and righteous man who had been looking for the Kingdom of God, but whose final tribute could be nothing more than shroud and tomb.

Contrary Evidence Now

Contrary evidence has always been in rich supply. Promises the Bible makes about the triumph of the Kingdom seem nothing more than that — promises, promises, or hype delivered like commercials during timeouts in the game of life. Trumpets that herald the coming of the king are out of tune with what is really happening in the world. The nightly news is bleak. Our medical reports suggest that God must be a little less than caring, loving, and available for help. And the little kingdom each of us had hoped to build skids out of our control and crashes like an auto on a slippery slope in wintery Minnesota.

The church, frequently it seems, has little more to offer. The lust for power, honor, glory that has been the character of people everywhere has not been lost within her pale. We struggle to achieve greatness, put in our bids in not-so-subtle ways for seats of honor in the Kingdom. There are dirty-tricks campaigns that scatter victims on their way. Impatient with the impact of the Gospel, we try to make the Kingdom come on our terms, not on Christ's, by power plays instead of meekness movements. The mission is contemporized to make folks feel good about themselves, to win friends and influence people at the expense of other people. Vaunted claims of inclusiveness result in subtle exclusiveness. Sin is upgraded to the level of "that's how it is these days," and forgiveness is a word reserved for pious liturgies. In ways like these, and many others, we try to make a mark, increase the numbers by decreasing faith's commitment, win people to the rolls of membership without the cost, manage programs of social improvement that are blowing in the wind without concern for spiritual growth. The last thing we would look for is a crucifixion. If *he* could not save *him*self, *we* ought at least to save *our*selves.

Where is Now Your God?

Where is now your God? He is on the cross. His Majesty the King is crowned with glory now. Execution day has become his coronation day, for nowhere does the glory of the Lord appear to faith more brightly than at Calvary. To faith, I said, the conviction of things not seen, until you believe it. The hidden, not the obvious; the revealed, not the discovered; the foolishness, not the wisdom.

The glory of the Lord is not without its witness, for from the strangest source the tribute to the king is heard: "Lord, remember me when you come into your kingdom."

As the death grip tightened on the malefactor crucified with Christ, the prospect triggered instant replays of his wasted life. As a partner in disorganized crime he had received the reward of merit and within the hour his biography, ignoble as it was, would close. With the little strength yet left to him, he rebuked the mocking malefactor on the other cross, then turned to Jesus with his final plea, offering this last remnant of his misspent years, the only moments that could still be salvaged.

We cannot know what Dismas, as tradition names him, could have heard or known of Christ before this intimate experience at Calvary as partner in the crucifixion. But as his mental VCR rolled off the record of his life, there could be no other cry but mercy. There was no more evidence for Dismas than there is for us that Jesus was indeed a king, or that his execution was a coronation, but in a way that only grace can tell, his eyes of faith were opened to behold a love the world had never seen, and in that love to find his only hope.

And hope was realized. In those last moments of this life our Lord established a relationship with Dismas to endure for all eternity, "Today you shall be with me in paradise." There is no way to account for this except that God moves in with us just as we are, not as we ought to be, includes us in his Kingdom by his grace, because he loves, and because in grace and love his cross is our forgiveness. Believe it, then you'll see it.

Do we need it? Sister, Brother, do we need it! I know that modern woman and modern man try to handle sin and guilt in other ways. Deny it! Excuse it, defend it, pass it off to others. The mood today is one that scarcely understands the terms. Even this good word "malefactor," for example, is a pulpit word that no one understands. Troublemaker, thug, thief, rapist, mugger might probably be better. But for whatever ill may be our character, are we responsible? Hardly! Society is the culprit for doing it to us. We were born that way. Peer pressures laid it on us. Or we did what our hearts told us to do, and we were told that if it feels good, we could do it, so we did it.

But the modern folks I know, and you know, too, are kissing cousins to those other modern men and women that we meet in Genesis and Exodus. They have all the symptoms of being unforgiven.

In contrast, one of those modern women in the Scriptures who was a sinner, heard the word, "Your sins are forgiven." A modern chiseler down in Jericho was told, "Today salvation has come to this house," and he was forgiven. A modern victim of paralysis at Bethesda heard the word of the Lord, "Rise, take up your pad and walk." A modern victim of a modern scourge who asked for mercy and for cleansing by the will of God was told, "I will. Be clean." And to this dying thief, another modern, came the promise, "Today you shall be with me in paradise." Astonishing! Astonishing as grace!

What was it Jesus said to you? To me? When he enfolds that cherished little lamb of yours within the bosom of his Kingdom at the font of Baptism, "Your sins are forgiven." When he reaches out for us around his table, "Your sins are forgiven." When he speaks the word of promise to our guilt-stressed hearts, "Your sins are forgiven." And at every turn he holds the cross before our faith, for it is there that his forgiving grace becomes reality, and there the glory of his love reveals a king and kingdom that can be revealed no other way. Forgiven! Believe it, then you'll see it. You will see his crucifixion as his coronation, and as he crowns you with the gift of everlasting life, you will bring the royal diadem to crown him Lord of all, and your Lord, your king, too.

"There they crucified him, and the criminals, one on the right and one on the left." And we recall before we leave this crucifixion scene that we, too, have been crucified with Christ. We died with him. The hopelessness of our bad situations, the guilt of sin, the power of death, the fear-filled future — these have all been stripped of their destructive powers by the Power on the throne. We, too, today, will be with him in paradise, and the crucifixion scene will become our coronation scene, for he who believes in him *has* everlasting life. Believe it, and you will see it.

John 12:9-19   *Christ the King (C)*

Christ is King

Today we have the privilege of a preview of that glory when eternity begins, when every knee shall bend and every tongue confess that Jesus Christ is Lord, to the glory of the Father. The day is *Christ the King*, the final Sunday in another round of time with Christ. We can hear the trumpet of the seventh angel, and the voices loudly shouting in the heavens (Apocalypse 11:15), "The kingdom of this world has become the kingdom of our Lord and of his Christ, and he shall reign forever and ever." We are in the company of the twenty-four elders who sit on their thrones before God, and who fall on their faces to worship him, saying,

> *We give thanks to thee, O Lord God almighty, that thou hast taken thy great power and begun to reign.*

We need not reserve our praises for the glory of eternity. We praise him now. "Lift every voice and sing, Glory to Christ our king!" This one more word we need to say, this one more thing we need to do on this last Sunday of the year: "Crown him Lord of all," for *Christ is King*. The nations are his heritage. The ends of the earth are his possession. If a psalmist centuries ago could recognize that, why can't we? But whether we say yea or nay, the fact will never change. "Be wise, O kings; be warned, O rulers of the earth." Serve the Lord with awe, respect, and fear. Rejoice, you people of the living God, for you are blessed as you take refuge in your Christ. One day you will behold by sight what you have owned by faith.

Wondrous Sovereign

Recently a cruise line operating in the Caribbean launched a cruise ship billed as the most luxurious, most dazzling, and the largest of its kind. It boasts four miles of corridors that lead to staterooms, dining rooms, boutiques, two cinemas, lounges, casinos, and bars, and an ambience that truly reflects the American lifestyle. The ship was christened *Sovereign of the Seas.*

That the name reflects our lifestyle there will be no doubt. The sovereign lords we choose are those that dazzle us with glitter, that promise an adventure in the comfort culture with the finest cuisine, that appeal to status interests, that provide a respite in luxury from the stress of the daily grind. Paul Gerhardt's hymn line is passé when he describes the Christ as he "who points the clouds their courses, whom winds and waves obey." And even some of our more contemporary lines, "Ruler of wind and wave," "Whose arm has bound the restless wave," — seem musty as we marvel at the mighty ships of luxury that cruise the seas. Once upon a time there was a *Titanic.*

As a child I found my mother's joy in the piano lessons she provided for her sons so that one of them could play for her the gospel hymns she loved to sing on winter evenings. I remember in particular the one we never missed. It had the line, "Wondrous Sovereign of the sea, Jesus, Savior, pilot me." Too bad we lost it in our high church passion for the perfect hymn. Although less than forty miles from the beaches of Lake Michigan, we had never seen a sea, but we knew what it meant, this Edward Hopper line, and it would stand us in good stead through boisterous waves and hiding rocks and treacherous shoal of life. Some of those waves were more than boisterous, and some of those rocks were mighty hard, but the pilot never failed us.

We have often left the sovereignty of God to Calvinists for accent, and therefore we have frequently made molehills out of mountains, reducing the majesty of God to the level of our mini-worship, awe to irreverence, obedience to insolence, honor and respect to impudence. But today we bend stiff knees and loosen our tied tongues and raise our spiritually-arthritic arms to wave the palms of victory. "Hosanna. Blessed is he who comes in the name of the Lord, even the King of Israel!"

Glory in Strange Places

The Word is in the Gospel according to Saint John, that Fourth Gospel where the glory of the Lord appears in strange places. John paints the scene of Jesus' entry to the Holy City with a different brush than Matthew uses, or Mark, or Luke. For Jesus came here, as his word predicted, to be crucified, but in that curcifixion to be glorified. In the Gospel as John writes it the cross is not a tragedy, but triumph, not a gory scene, but glory scene, for here as nowhere else the glory of God's love breaks through. It is in the cross that Jesus glorifies the Father and the Father glorifies his Son, defeats the demon world of death and brings the life abundant, breaks the power brokers of this world with a rod of iron and dashes them in pieces like a potter's vessel, and establishes his Kingdom evermore. The glory of the cross!

In the Gospel of Saint John, therefore, we find much less of the bizarre that marks our Lord's triumphal entry to the city, the meekness and the lowliness of this parade that in the other Gospels prompted many in the crowd to ask, "Who is this?" "What strange business is this?" We remember that we have the picture of a coronation scene in this triumphal march akin to that when Solomon succeeded to the throne of David, and when his coronation culminated in a great procession through the city streets as Solomon, the Lord's anointed, rode his mule and people shouted, "Long live Solomon, the king of Israel." We can hear the echo of that ancient chant, "Fear not, daughter of Zion; behold your king is coming, sitting on an ass's colt." An ass's colt? Of course. They had no

Lincoln Continentals. And the people cried, "Hosanna! Blessed is he who comes in the name of the Lord, even the king of Israel."

Notice how Saint John lines up events that immediately preceded Jesus' journey to Jerusalem from Bethany, around the Mount of Olives. The chapter just ahead of this records the story of the Savior's kingship over death, the raising of his good friend Lazarus at Bethany, one who had been ill and who had died, whom Jesus summoned from the tomb and freed not only from the grave clothes but the chains of death itself.

There were many who believed, while others served as bugging devices in the embassy and hastened to the Pharisees with their report of what had happened. But again the kingship of our Lord reveals itself, for the prophecy of Caiaphas, "It is expedient for you that one should die," became a prophecy placed on his lips by Christ the King himself, "for he did not say this of his own accord, but being high priest that year, he prophesied that Jesus should die for the nation, and not for the nation only, but to gather into one the children of God who are scattered abroad." For the hour had come for the Son of man to be glorified, to take his power and reign.

The curious crowd to whom the word had spread rushed out to Bethany to gawk. They had to see it for themselves, not only Jesus, but this Lazarus whom he had called forth from the tomb. Do you mean it really happened? A man was dead and now he lives? And on the next day when they heard that he was coming into town to celebrate the Passover, they gathered in the streets with palms to meet him and to hail him as the king. We like that kind of king.

Then John adds the usual commentary, "His disciples did not understand this at first, but when Jesus was glorified, then they remembered."

I think we can be sympathetic toward the twelve disciples, for it can be said of us as well, "His disciples did not understand at first." How little we understand. But is it necessary that we understand? It is more important to believe, even though we cannot understand. The nightly news in those days was as bleak and dismal as it is in ours. To understand that Christ is king would take some doing then, as now. The evidence is all contrary.

No Royal Trappings

The royal trappings in the life and ministry of Christ were conspicuous by absence. He owned no royal castle, occupied no royal throne, wore no royal robes. His associates did not include the upper echelon of royalty nor any of the hot shots people like to claim as friends. They were from the ranks of the poor, the oppressed, the captive. His attendants were selected from the fisher folk and tax collectors in a province the important people scorned. When he died, he had nothing but a rag to leave behind.

But is there evidence of royal trappings in his reign today? Is there anything to suggest that Christ is in control — in the world of war, or in this imperfect church, or in the pain and pressure and disaster of our personal empires where foundations shake and shatter? Does not the evidence suggest the question, "Where is now your God?" Has your king deserted you, or lost control, or has he been impeached, deposed, sent packing for conduct that betrays his office?

The disciples felt that way when in the week that followed they saw Jesus delivered into the hands of evil people, bound, and judged, and crucified. They could hardly understand that Friday as "Good" Friday. They scattered to the winds. Peter followed in shame and Judas took the sword and all of them forsook their master, save this good man John. Even the creation quaked and rumbled, and the sun refused to shine. Hope seemed shattered. Faith seemed trampled. The Hosanna to the king was lost amid the cries of "Crucify!"

The cross will not be seen as glory, nor the Christ as king, through the lens of media cameras or on reporters' note pads. Several members of the *Sixty Minutes* team of CBS-TV appeared some time ago before a luncheon meeting of the downtown chamber in our city. In the question period that followed the commentary from the team, someone asked, "What person in world history would you most like to interview?" One suggested Moses, of whom he would ask, "Why ten?" Another offered Jackie Robinson, the symbol of a new beginning in the world of baseball. But then another answered, "Jesus. He talked pretty good, and we might get fifteen minutes out of him." Several other comments about Jesus brought alternating groans and laughs, so that the writer of the news account was forced to add the comment that several in the audience were clearly offended.*

This Palm Sunday happening would certainly have been a media event to keep the camera crews around all week. But the possibility of interview was open to some question, for our Lord consistently refused to be subjected to the questions of the curious who saw no more in him than a good story. Nor would he get his foot caught in the traps that questioners would ask. There were those who tried to interview him — Caiaphas, King Herod, Pontius Pilate — but none of them would get a quarter hour.

There is another lens through which to view the cross. We see it through the lens of Easter's resurrection. He lives! Christ lives! The king has claimed the throne.

I cannot offer you a set of scientific facts to prove it, or a history book to demonstrate it, or a formula with which to test it. I can only give you Christ himself. The only proof that you will have, the only history that can demonstrate it, or the formula with which to test it, is in your own biography from here on out as one of his own subjects, living under him and in his kingdom. For that we have his promise.

*Reported in the *Minneapolis Star and Tribune,* October 28, 1986

Luke 17:11-19 *Thanksgiving Eve / Day*

One Nation, Under Mercy

Days of gratitude have been a long tradition on this continent. A group of settlers who arrived in Maine in 1607 held a service of thanksgiving for a safe journey to these shores. William Bradford of the Plymouth Colony proclaimed a special day of gratitude to the Almighty God when the settlers gathered in a bounteous harvest. The Battle of Saratoga was commemorated, at the orders of the Continental Congress, with a day of thanksgiving, the first time all the colonies observed the day together. Washington at Valley Forge and Lincoln in the midst of the Civil War proclaimed a nationwide observance of thanksgiving. Throughout our history, both in the United States and Canada, the tradition has continued in unbroken sequence. And this year again by presidential proclamation we observe this day as our Thanksgiving Day.

Thanksgiving is a national holiday, not necessarily a holy day. The church lifts up its heart and voice to God in Jesus Christ with gratitude in every liturgy, and in particular when gathered for the Holy Eucharist, a term which means thanksgiving. We give thanks for all his mighty acts with which the centuries of history since creation have been punctuated, for the promise given Abraham that has unfolded to fulfillment down the years in Jesus Christ, for the Holy Spirit and the living faith that he has breathed on us. We give thanks for the bounty of his blessing, for the special care he gives his people, for the fellowship of prophets and apostles and the Holy Catholic Church, and for all the company of heaven. All this is marked by mercy flowing through all aspects of our relationship with God — the forgiveness of sins, the assurance of the kingdom, and the solid hope of everlasting life.

But it is right and proper that we also gather in our house of worship on this holiday and make of it a holy day, that we join our fellow citizens in every state and province in expressing gratitude for this good earth and this good land, for the harvest, for the advances of science, for the research teams in laboratories, for the artists in our culture. With all who can't forget the source from whom our blessings flow, we thank our God for family and friends, for life and health, and even for the burdens of the moment that are always filtered through the fingers of a loving God to bring us good. It is right and proper that the people of this nation, ourselves among them, thank God with one heart and one voice.

Not everyone agrees with that. But even if the day is nothing but an opportunity for family fun and feast and football, a break in the routine of daily work, yet I believe that only the most cold and heartless feel no swell of gratitude. Generally it can be said that we are well-mannered people who have learned to squeeze a thank-you from our teeth and lips occasionally, and who have to be polite enough to those who favor us with graces and to those who don't, to say "Gratias, danke sehr, merci beaucoup, toda raba, or shokran" when a favor has been shown. But we need this lesson of the word today before the depths of gratitude are fully sounded, that we are

One Nation, Under Mercy

Under Mercy! Underscore that word, for mercy is the key to our thanksgiving as we bring it to the surface from the depths. So enter now again these ten from whom we have heard before, ten lepers somewhere near the border of Samaria and Galilee. In the context of a national holiday, and with fresh memories of the lady in the harbor, I recall the poetry of Emma Lazarus, *The New Colossus*, inscribed at the base of the Statue of Liberty,

> *Not like the giant of Greek fame,*
> *With conquering limbs astride from land to land!*
> *Here at our sea-washed, sunset gates shall stand*
> *A mighty woman with a torch, whose flame*
> *Is the imprisoned lightning, and her name*
> *Mother of exiles. From her beacon-hand*
> *Glows world-wide welcome; her mild eyes command*
> *The air-bridged harbor that twin cities frame.*
> *"Keep, ancient lands, your storied pomp!" cries she*
> *With silent lips. "Give me your tired, your poor,*
> *Your huddled masses yearning to breathe free,*
> *The wretched refuse of your teeming shore.*
> *Send them, the homeless, tempest-tost to me,*
> *I lift my lamp beside the golden door."*

Certainly in these ten lepers we can see the huddled masses yearning to breathe free, the tired, the poor. In their sad state they were now homeless, a wretched refuse of society condemned to spend the balance of their lives in caves of isolation, crying out "Unclean!" whenever anyone approached them. It was a living death they suffered, or worse, a living hell, beyond the cure of anything that Dr. Luke would have in his black leather bag or on his prescription list.

The Stranger and the Foreigner

And one of them was a stranger. Although it has been said that natural enemies find fellowship in common problems, or that the Jews and the Samaritans became friends against their common enemy of leprosy, I think that this might not be true. If there was anything as bad as leprosy, or worse, it would have been contamination by this hated foreigner. Even though they had to find a common isolated area in which to spend the balance of their days, a common cave in which to sleep, I think that for this one Samaritan it was a double whammy. And when they came to Jesus, as he neared them, crying not "Unclean," but "Jesus, Master, have mercy," I visualize this lone Samaritan as tagging on behind. If the nine could hope for mercy, perhaps there might be mercy for him, too, if he could just get close enough. Perhaps a little mercy might spill over onto him.

The ideals spelled out in the poem of Emma Lazarus, a welcome for the stranger and the foreigner, a haven for the huddled masses yearning to breathe free, new life for the wretched refuse of the nations — these ideals may not have been entirely attained. Strong resistance was encountered when our doors were opened to the refugees of Southeast Asia, and when the people of the church whose hearts had learned compassion at the cross of Christ assumed the role of sponsors in this land. When Fidel Castro opened prison cells and sent the wretched refuse of his land, they were not extended a warm welcome. But Jesus never spurned the stranger or the foreigner, the publican, the sinner, the Samaritan, the Galilean, the deaf, the blind, the handicapped, not even unclean lepers, not even thugs and thieves and prostitutes and criminals. Responding to their plea for mercy, Jesus said:

- to the prostitute, "Neither do I condemn you. Sin no more."
- to the deaf, "Ephatha! Be opened!"
- to the handicapped, "Arise, take up your bed and walk."
- to the dying thief, "Today you will be with me in paradise."
- and to these lepers, "Go, show yourselves to the priests."

When the Lord saw all this agony and fear and helplessness, he had compassion — not a passive pity, but an active love.

And as they went, they were healed. The story is familiar now. We teach it to the beginner class in Sunday School so that they will learn to be polite and say their thank you's. We act enraged by those nine lepers who, when cleansed, did not acknowledge him who cleansed. Or we put the story on the shelf as one whose lessons have been obvious and so well mastered that they need no more attention!

Mercy is the Key

Mercy, that's the key. Anyone who suffered leprosy would cry for mercy. But the nine were members of the chosen people, children of the covenant. If they were as we are in our similar reverses, they must have often questioned as we do, "Why me?" If parents owe it to their children to provide for them, protect them, nurture them, does not God owe it to us to protect us from this scourge and all the scourges that afflict the human race? He promised. We are special, as he said, but to be smitten in this way is hardly special treatment. In *our* book the word is merit, not mercy. God *owes* it to us.

For if God made us in his image, and if he promised to be faithful to us as his children, what right does he have to see us maimed or cancered, starving for want of bread, struggling with food stamps, clobbered by a bad economy, handicapped by loss of limb or sight or audio? He created human beings to be human. Therefore, let him see to it that we are truly and fully human. These are our human rights — to be fed, to be prosperous, to be whole. If someone has to be afflicted, let it be the stranger and the foreigner halfway around the world, or the sinner who is always swinging on his own, but not at our house, please.

In the Midst of Abundance

There is an attitude that floats the surface of American civil religion, that supposes that we are a chosen people on this continent, singled out for special favors for our special status as Canadians and Americans. The richest nations of the world? Obviously, why not? God promised it, God owes it to us. Superpower in the world? Obviously, why not? Has not God chosen us to be the guardians and protectors and police force in the earth, and isn't there just wage for such responsibility? The word we use is merit, not mercy. Gratitude is difficult in the midst of the abundance, and mercy is a strange word on the lips of those who feel abundance is their right. Well, Jesus did say that he came to bring life, and that we might have life abundantly, but he did not say it was our *right* to have abundance. He did intimate, in fact, that when abundance is our style, and when the landfills are choked with our throw-away, the abundant life is often dimmed. How hard it is for those who have abundance to enter the kingdom of heaven. Remember the camel squeezing through the needle's eye?

No, the word is mercy. So this lone stranger, the Samaritan, returned with thanks. He knew the key word, mercy. He knew he had no claim on God, no claim on Christ. Nor did he have the right as a Samaritan to show himself to the priests, for they would have ordered him begone and they would have no truck with him. So he returned to Jesus, falling on his face before him, and praising *God*. He saw the mercy he had begged for as the mercy of God that had come to him through Jesus Christ. He returned not only to give thanks for healing at the word of Jesus, but to praise God who had first come to him in Jesus. Incarnate in the Christ, the mercy of the Lord of heaven and earth!

"Ten sickly lepers all in a row. Nine men were healed. One was made whole."

At the Easter Vigil just a few years back, I had the joy of serving as the Holy Spirit's instrument in the baptism of thirty-five Hmong persons, refugees from northern Laos, people who had crossed the Mekong River in the dead of night, escaped a shower bath of bullets, then from the camps in Thailand came to a new home in the United States. It had not been easy to communicate with them in preparation for their baptism, but they had learned to know this word, *mercy*. And we who worked with them could only help them to identify that word with Jesus Christ.

In a sequel to that story, a man who represented parish leadership was heard to comment as he left the service that he would never be around for anything like that again. He had better things to do on Easter eve. But in contrast there was

Mary, whose heart spilled out compassion like water from a sponge, and who together with a company of other Spirit-born assumed the sponsorship in this new homeland for these desperate refugees. As the candidates for baptism stepped forward one by one. Mary stood beside me at the font and sorted out for me those thirty-five strange-sounding names that were then being written in the Book of Life and given their inheritance as children of the heavenly Father. Mary and the others had themselves experienced mercy. Could that be the reason? There had been strange-sounding names before, on people who found refuge on these shores — German names, Norwegian names, Swedish names, and Irish names. Now there were names like Va, and Nou, and Houa.

Get on, then, with your Thanksgiving Day. We eat today, not by merit, but by mercy. We enjoy our families today, not by merit, but by mercy. We revel in abundance, not by merit, but by mercy. We can enjoy the heroics of our football gladiators on the tube this afternoon, if that's our thing, not by merit, but by mercy. What other blessings would you like to mention?

Let each of us in our thanksgiving voice our gratitude not for the things that can so easily be stripped away from us, or for the things we have accumulated through the years that are dead weight on life, but for the mercy of our God. And forget it not this national holiday: we are one nation, under mercy. This whole blessed nation is "under God," indeed — but under God *in mercy*!

www.ingramcontent.com/pod-product-compliance
Lightning Source LLC
Chambersburg PA
CBHW060845050426
42453CB00008B/839